BIG IDEA PATTERNS
CREATIVITY TOOLKIT FOR EVERY ARTIST

CABE LINDSAY

FOREWARD BY MARIA RIVERA

Ahstin

AHSTIN BOOKS

BALLYHOO

"Opening the gate of fresh ideas is not a thinking but a doing. Techniques such as the ones expanded in this book are very useful, and if your creativity engine is stuck you'll find that it is much easier to get it going if you feed it with a different kind of fuel first."

—Sebastien Gendry
Founder of Laughter Wellness
LaughterWellness.org

"Cabe Lindsay's book, *Big Idea Patterns*, sheds new light on the creative process that all designers must go through to create that 'ah-hah' moment. This book explores the process of generating 'big ideas' with step-by-step formulas. I highly recommend this book as a vehicle to reexamine our own methods of creativity and how to improve upon them."

—Frederick Graber
Creative Director, i2i Group
i2iGroup.net

"I experienced Cabe Lindsay's creativity first hand when he took the Creative Strategy and Execution Class I taught in the Department of Advertising and Public Relations at Michigan State University. We had great discussions and debates about creativity and "big ideas." I was so impressed with Cabe that I invited him to be the TA for the class the following semester where he helped teach other students how to discover and develop their big ideas. I was honored to provide Cabe with a letter of recommendation when he applied for graduate school to continue his studies. I have watched him climb into the art director's role, and I am proud to see that he continues to inspire others as a writer. *Big Idea Patterns* is a toolset full of classic and innovative strategies for brainstorming and jumpstarting the creative engine, guaranteed to get people revved up about big ideas"

—Dr. William J. Ward a.k.a. DR4WARD
Social Media Professor, Syracuse University
S.I. Newhouse School of Public Communications
Newhouse.Syr.edu

"Big ideas are driven by great purpose. If you are looking for ways to discover your big idea and articulate it in a way that inspires people, the patterns in this book will help you. I know because Cabe and patterns in this book have helped us at InXero to inspire channel-centric businesses to become engines of growth. We believe every business is a sun."

—Anand Raj

Founder and CEO, InXero

InXero.com

"Lindsay lays down a comprehensive groundwork for the creative process based on hard research. Then comes the most important thing; he has fun with it."

—Nate Stine

Copywriter, lookthinkmake

lookthinkmake.com

"In *Big Idea Patterns* Cabe Lindsay removes the shroud of mystery from the creative process. Ever accessible and interesting, Lindsay deciphers the fundamentals of creativity by introducing readers to a medley of time-tested techniques and novel approaches backed by sound research and personal experience. This is essential reading for anyone looking to harness their creative energy!"

—Kevin D. Thomas

Assistant Professor, The University of Texas at Austin

Department of Advertising and Public Relations

Advertising.UTexas.edu

BIG IDEA PATTERNS

CREATIVITY TOOLKIT FOR EVERY ARTIST

Big Idea Patterns: Creativity Toolkit. First published in the United States of America by Ahstin™ 2013. For information address the publisher: Ahstin Books, Austin, TX, USA. Details at Ahstin.com.

ISBN-13: 978-0615896618 (Ahstin)
ISBN-10: 0615896618

BigIdeaPatterns.com

DEDICATION

To my mentors: Lori Darley, Joan Sheski, and Maria Rivera.

TABLE OF CONTENTS

FOREWARD

The "C" word scares people. "Creativity" implies having a rare and mystical gift bestowed upon only a select few. But what if we shifted our thinking into allowing it versus having it? Being open to it rather than being it?

I traveled to Cuba in April, having only been once— ten years before. Both times, I was amazed by the Cubans' resourcefulness. In a country where scarcity is abundant and manufacturing is virtually non-existent, ideas for how to "resolver," as they say in Spanish, or "solve/make do" are not. So little gets thrown out. The old (car, watch, bicycle) is simply made new. (Or newer.) Or transformed and reframed altogether. Creative problem solving is a daily requirement in a country where living with less is a daily reality. It is a natural response rather than a high-pressured edict.

By practicing the art of capturing creativity (jotting down the flash of inspiration, holding on to the source of an idea in tangible ways), we approach it. Ignore nothing and live fully awake. What if, like the lightning bugs we caught in the past, cupping our hands together so as to see the glow, creativity needs simply to be caught? It's already there.

And it's here. In the book you're about to dive into. Read, learn, but also live the lessons...go do, see, taste, run, love, and then, let creativity reveal itself in ways that are true for you.

Be bold. It is said that "fortune favors the brave." So, too, does creativity favor the curious and the courageous.

—Maria Rivera, September 11, 2013
Texas Creative Instructor, 2005-2013
The University of Texas at Austin

CHAPTER 1
UNDERSTANDING CREATIVITY

Creativity is a birthright, for some of us. Like owlets, able to fly on the first try, occasional artists are born wise. Some of us learn to fall before we learn to fly, more like squirrels, while still others claim to have no hope in flying, like fish. But flying fish do exist, you know. The truth is this: creativity can be learned, practiced, and developed. From the preschool level to the university level and beyond, all of us can realize our creative potential. We all have the ability to tap into the clouds of the subconscious, where creativity lives. Consider this guidebook a cloud-tapping toolkit.

Creativity is a valued asset. The admiration of creativity in the U.S. is illustrated in a *Time* magazine article, revealing that 94% of Americans value creativity in others. Creativity is valued above intelligence, 93%, compassion, 92%, humor, 89%, ambition, 88%, and beauty, 57%. Yes, and 65% think creativity is central to America's role as a global leader (Kluger, 2013). Author Richard Florida claims that a

"Creative Age" is the driving force behind America's economic recovery, led by a creative class of 40 million creative professionals—30% of the U.S. workforce—including educators, entertainers, architects, engineers, and others whose primary responsibility is to "create meaningful new forms" (Florida, 2012).

This is a time of impressively high regard for big ideas. In fact, creativity and innovation are the top ranked priorities for businesses, according to Boston Consulting Group's annual strategy survey (Andrew, Manget, Michael, Taylor, & Zablit, 2010). Further proof is in the fact that as of 2012, for the second consecutive year, the word "creative" is the most commonly used buzzword on LinkedIn—the social networking website for people in professional occupations. Individuals today value creativity above all else. Nations today depend on innovation to drive their economic upswings and solve their crises. Creativity rules.

Research studies demonstrate the need for creativity in today's workplace everywhere from the developed countries to the developing countries, and from the individual to the organization as a whole. A recent United Nations report states that creative industries are stimulating economic recovery, globally. For example, exports of creative goods and services more than doubled between 2002-2008, during a time of recession and world crises (UNCTAD, 2010).

Evidence that creativity is part of our everyday work is the 2009 NESTA Everyday Innovation survey proposing that creativity is an integral part of modern work. Truly, creative problem-solving is a responsibility shared by every professional, from the shop floor to the cubicle, and from the executive computer to the artist's canvas (Patterson, Kerrin, Gatto-Roissard, & Coan, 2009).

Sociologists argue that the emerging creative class holds the potential for radically reshaping the attitudes and material realities of American life. *The Cultural Creatives: How 50 Million People Are Changing the World* is a nonfiction social sciences book that coined the term "Cultural Creatives" to describe one quarter of the American adult population. By definition, cultural creatives approach the world with enlightened creativity. Their characteristics include: involvement in creating a new and better way of life, and awareness of planet-wide issues, i.e. climate change, poverty, etc. Their values include: interconnectedness, altruism, self-actualization, and authenticity (Ray & Anderson, 2000).

Spinning off the *Cultural Creatives* book is the marketing consumer book, *Karma Queens, Geek Gods and Innerpreneurs*. Here, the authors identify a highly creative subculture in entrepreneurship: "innerpreneurs." Innerpreneurs have the defining characteristics of a cultural creative entrepreneur: high need for achievement, independence, and opportunity; low need for conformity, and propensity for risk-taking. Unlike yesterday's entrepreneurs who use their business solely for monetary gain, today's innerpreneurs use their business for personal fulfillment, resulting in creative expression and social change (Rentel & Zellnik, 2007). The existence of innerpreneurs and cultural creatives in this world is a sign that things are changing in ways favorable for the entire planet.

And the best news of all is that we can all be artists. Creative skills can be learned, exercised, and improved with the goal of achieving creative freedom. True of any art form, becoming a master artist begins with awareness, transitions through trial and error, moves into finesse, and improves over time through practice. Like all processes, the creative process is a series of steps taken in order to achieve a goal. For the purposes of this book, the goal in advancing along the path of the creative process is to achieve big ideas. This book aims to prove that every person is capable of discovering big ideas for themselves, and creativity is a skillset that can be developed, through awareness and practice. The purpose of this book is twofold: (1) enable artists with tools that will help them to become productive, and prolific; and (2) encourage people in their artistic aspirations.

This book recognizes three steps in the idea seeker's journey: (1) adapting to the behavior patterns best suited for creativity; (2) understanding the essential techniques for ideation; and (3) finding the resources that carry ideas into action. Within the behavior patterns, techniques, and resources advocated in this book, a resourceful set of tools is given. These tools can be observed, tested, and measured in terms of their problem-solving effectiveness, granting artists the ability to track their progress and find out which tools fit best. It is simple to see the benefit of familiarizing oneself with a creativity toolset, and there is tremendous value in streamlining creativity—it may be the cure for writer's block.

This guidebook aims to make artists prolific and end writer's block once and for all, by giving creative professionals a clear understanding of creative processes. With the creativity toolset given here, anyone can improve his or her ability to imagine, invent, create, and communicate big ideas. This book shows readers how to discover big ideas systematically. There are specific behavior patterns that clearly define successful artists and there are techniques and resources that writers commonly use to arrive at big ideas. Some of these behaviors, techniques, and resources are well-known and time-tested, while others are proposed here for the first time, backed by research and first-hand experience.

Enhancing the productivity of creativity is possible by improving the potency of "ideation," i.e. idea formulation. Building this model for ideation begins with an assessment of existing research in the area of creativity as it relates to advertising and other creative professions. The research findings in this book lead to a showcase of today's emerging creative professionals, highlighting the artistic traits of tomorrow's marketplace. Next, the creative process is examined, first by analyzing behavior patterns of advanced artists compared to beginners, and then exploring the techniques and resources available to artists. After that is a look at some remarkably big ideas and the action steps that have made them explode.

Researching Creativity

A study of creative processes logically begins with a definition of creativity. The two essential elements that define creativity are as follows: newness and value. To an advertising specialist, creativity is viewed as a way to smartly address complicated problems for the benefit of a client (Goldenberg & Mazursky, 2002). As stated by psychologists Mumford, Hunter, and Byrne (2009), creativity results in "the production of original, high quality, and elegant solutions to novel, complex, ill-defined problems" (Mumford, Hunter, & Byrne, 2009). By *Wikipedia* (2010) creativity is defined as follows:

> Creativity refers to the phenomenon whereby a
> person creates something new (a product, a

solution, a work of art, etc.) which has some kind of value. What counts as "new" may be in reference to the individual creator, or to the society or domain within which the novelty occurs.

Information available here includes a review of available research and a summary of findings, leading to big idea patterns that cultivate creative thought. This information is valuable because creativity is generally unexplainable—it is often random and sporadic (Goldenberg, Mazursky, & Solomon, 1999). For the same reason, research on the topic of creative processes is uncommon. Frankly, there is no go-to method that works every time for all people. However, there are indeed behavior patterns, techniques and resources that have proven rewarding in discovering big ideas. These are collected here as an advanced brainstorming guidebook, serving artists, writers, inventors, architects, and all other creative professionals as the atlas to the clouds of their ideas.

CHAPTER 2
BIG IDEAS = BIG VALUE

"The true sign of intelligence is not knowledge but imagination." —Albert Einstein

"Curiosity about life in all of its aspects, I think, is still the secret of great creative people." —Leo Burnett

The measure of a big idea's strength stems from its originality and appropriateness. Unoriginal ideas fall short as being uninspired and commonplace, while off-target ideas fall short as being tactless or irrelevant. When critiquing a big idea, the presence of originality and appropriateness is crucial, and a balance in these is desirable. At their extreme, some ideas are overly emotional or offbeat, likely producing expressions that lack substance or selling points. On the flip-side, some ideas are overly logical, thus being pedantic, producing boring, factual, "hard sell" expressions. Therefore, the goal for a creative professional is to ensure that the creative expression appeals to both sides of an audience's intellect in a balanced way (Barry, 2008) (Kilgour & Koslow, 2009).

To focus an artist's creative efforts and ensure the ideas are as appropriate as they are original, advertising agencies have developed models for defining the creative strategy. The Leo Burnett Company's advertising strategy model is one of the best known formulas. The Leo Burnett Company's fill-in-the-blanks model originated with its client, Procter & Gamble, and is widely used today for writing a creative strategy:

[Big idea] will [verb] [target audience] that [featured object] equals [advantage]. Support will be [rationale]. Tone will be [adjectives].

The Leo Burnett Company's advertising strategy model can be applied to any creative endeavor, with the benefit of focusing an artist's creativity.

There are three parts to a creative strategy: (1) objective statement; (2) support statement; and (3) tone of voice (Bendinger, 1993). The objective statement combines the mission statement with description of target audience, e.g. Advertising will convince conservative, low-income mothers, that apples are healthy children's snacks. The support statement substantiates or explains the reason why the product is beneficial, e.g. Support will be the high vitamin and fiber content. The tone of voice describes the selling attitude or long-term values of the brand, e.g. Tone of the message will be upbeat and sweet. Outside the context of advertising, the model might look as follows: Oil painting will convince folk art enthusiasts that apples are the most dangerous fruits in the woods. Support will be the apple's alarming red color, and the presence of a nearby raven, suggesting death. Tone will be dark and alluring.

The Advertising Profession

Fundamentally, in order for an idea to be considered valuable to an audience, it must be both original and appropriate, and this is particularly true in the advertising industry (Kilgour & Koslow, 2009). Advertising is the quintessential creative occupation. In advertising, the big idea is everything—a winning idea can engage an audience even with poor execution of art direction and copywriting, but even the most attractive words and imagery can't help a losing idea to shine (Ashley & Oliver, 2010). One cannot "polish the dirt to make a diamond," as the saying goes.

It has been said that creative people create, but they do not analyze, while analysts are analytical and not creative (Russell & Lane, 1996). However, the advertising profession is a notable exception—here, the job requires equal parts left-brain logic and right-brain creativity. On the analytical side, a big idea in advertising is one that appropriately reaches the right audience with the right message at the right time. On the creative side, a big idea in advertising is one that surprises the audience in an exciting and memorable way. This dual responsibility for originality and appropriateness falls upon the "creative director," whose duty is to ensure the value of an agency's creative output. It is essential for advertising artists to be well-equipped in both sides of the brain, and the same is likely true of all commercially-successful artists and writers.

Advancements in digital photography and digital filmmaking have simplified the recording of images. Alas, professional camera work still demands equal parts right- and left-brain intelligence: both rational and spontaneous decision-making.

Since creativity is of utmost importance in an advertising agency, the successful management of creativity is a surefire route to prosperity. Creative professionals often seek ways to become more productive as they progress from one creative task to another (Goldenberg, Mazursky, & Solomon, 1999). Ad agencies are the only organizations in which creativity is the primary service offering, and "Creative" is the name of a department headed by a "Creative Director." Creative thought is so valuable in ad agencies that entire business structures are sometimes designed around the talents of one bright mind (Tellis & Ambler, 2007). A strong handling of creative processes is essential to an ad agency's success in developing business-building ideas for their clients (McNamara, 1990) (Kilgour & Koslow, 2009).

On the subject of creative processes that are involved in the production of advertisements, only a small number of academic studies are available. Approximately two dozen relevant electronic articles exist in the libraries of the University of Texas at Austin. An *Amazon.com* search turned up around 10 books related directly to the subject, incl. David Ogilvy's *Ogilvy on Advertising*, with another 20 books indirectly related, incl. Daniel Pink's *A Whole New Mind: Why Right-Brainers Will Rule the Future.* This book is a collection of insights from the various perspectives of academic researchers and creative professionals. The objective is to reach emerging artists, writers, and advertising specialists with some positive reinforcement as well as a comprehensive tools of techniques and resources for discovering big ideas: a creativity toolkit.

At the heart of the development of marketing communications is the "big idea," described as: a contribution to a brand image in an original and appropriate way (Kilgour & Koslow, 2009). David Ogilvy, "The Father of Advertising," emphasized the weight of the big idea in his classic 1983 book, *Ogilvy on Advertising*, in which he writes that no idea is big unless it will work for 30 years. He adds, "Big ideas come from the subconscious. This is true in art, in science, and in advertising. But your subconscious has to be well informed, or your idea will be irrelevant" (Ogilvy, 1983).

David Ogilvy advises knowing as much as possible about a topic of interest to ensure on-target ideation of it. He says, "The more you know about it, the more likely you are to come up with a big idea for selling it." Ogilvy advocates research among test groups to find out how audience members respond to the product or service. In his experience, creative professionals benefit greatly from knowing what attributes are important to consumers and what promises are most likely to make the audience respond (Ogilvy, 1983). Modern creative directors agree. The more diverse one's knowledge is, the broader one's basis of intuition is—this leads artists to new connections and, ultimately, big ideas (White, 2002).

Solving the Pains of Creative Professions

Clearly, creativity is the definitive service delivered in creative professions, and big ideas are the highest goals. Definitely, big ideas must be relevant to their respective audience in order to bear any value. Sadly, originality and appropriateness can be difficult to achieve on demand.

Unfortunately, the mind is not easily tapped. It is unpredictable. It may not appear on command, and it "escapes most attempts at manipulation and control" (Ziegler & Johnson, 1981). On one occasion, ideas may flow freely and easily, while on another occasion, writer's block occurs. The idiosyncrasy of creativity is well-stated in a study by Tellis and Ambler (2007) on the subject of advertising management:

> Creativity may consist of overcoming the banal (sheer regularity) on one hand and the bizarre (sheer surprise) on the other; thus achieving a middle way between normativity and crazitivity, and enhancing effectiveness.

The advertising industry is an environment of tenacious competition. In this deadline-obsessed field, creative services must be delivered faster, more efficiently, with more impact, on budget and on time. (Ashley & Oliver, 2010). Performance-related issues are a top concern of advertising agencies, as return-on-investment is increasingly important to clients (Riveong, 2007). For example, a noteworthy trend in the client-agency relationship is the increasing termination of agencies that under-perform. The average client-agency relationship lasted over 7.2 years in 1984, and that number declined to 5.3 years by 1997 (American Association of Advertising Agencies, 2007).

The solution to all of these pain points is a systematized approach to ideation. Creative teams often seek ways to become more productive as they progress from one creative task to another (Goldenberg, Mazursky, & Solomon, 1999), and so it appears there is a wide demand for techniques and resources that streamline the creative process. Yes, a simplified route to big ideas is desirable to any creative professional. Imagine the efficiency in using the tools that consistently lead to productive ideas, while avoiding those that do not. A creativity toolkit is exactly what is needed.

- - - - - - - - - - ✂ -

Key Takeaways in Big Ideas = Big Value

- An idea is understandably valuably when it is balanced in its originality and appropriateness.
- Big ideas ideally appeal to both sides of an audience's intellect: logic and creativity.
  - Logical ideas deliver the right message at the right time, to the right audience.
  - Creative ideas surprise the audience in an exciting and memorable way.
- Advertising, for example, blends left-brain logic and right-brain creativity in order to satisfy clients.
  - A creative strategy helps to ensure that ideation is on-target as well as innovative.
- A streamlined, systematized approach to ideation solves the challenge of discovering big ideas on demand.

CHAPTER 3
DEFINING THE CREATIVE PROCESS

"When I am...completely myself, entirely alone, and of good cheer...it is on such occasions that my ideas flow best and most abundantly. Whence and how these ideas come I know not nor can I force them." —Wolfgang Amadeus Mozart

"You can't wait for inspiration, you have to go after it with a club." —Jack London

Leo Burnett is one of the most influential creative thinkers of the 20th century, as declared by *Time* magazine in 2010. His self-named advertising firm is perhaps most famous for creating memorable brand icons such as: the Jolly Green Giant, the Marlboro Man, and the Pillsbury Doughboy, to name a few. From his professional perspective, Burnett is quoted in Bendinger (1993) as follows: "Creativity is the art of establishing new and meaningful relationships between previously unrelated things...which somehow present the product in a fresh, new light." He proceeds, "The secret of all effective originality in advertising is not the creation of new and tricky words and pictures, but putting familiar words and pictures into new relationships."

Posing theories about creative processes is a complicated task, partly because creativity itself is an abstract and subjective concept. The process of generating new ideas is a subject area that has eluded researchers, with only a small number of exceptions. Literary publications pertaining to the creative process include works by advertising heroes, such as David Ogilvy (1983), as well as experienced educators, such as Professor John Philip Jones (1999). Systematic investigations related to the creative process have been led by: Goldenberg, Mazursky, and Solomon (1999); Koslow, Sasser, and Riordan (2006); and Sasser & Koslow (2008). These are the chief references that apply to the topic at hand—research on the subject of creative processes.

Research in creativity can be divided into three major perspectives, relating to: (1) the people who create; (2) the places or environments in which they work; and (3) the processes they follow in developing creative ideas (Sasser & Koslow, 2008). Previous research pertaining to *people* study models of individual creativity, attempting to gain insights into what makes individuals creative, i.e. how they are different from others. Previous research pertaining to the *place* focuses on the physical workspace and agency culture (Sasser & Koslow, 2008). This book is focused primarily on the *process*.

The *process* is the most mysterious aspect of creativity, according to some researchers (Sasser & Koslow, 2008). Research studies pertaining to the creative process often focus on factors involved with the production of creative advertising campaigns, for example. Analyses of creative processes aim to reveal the "artistic science" of creativity. For example, Goldenberg, Mazursky, and Solomon (1999) focus on advantages in a particular creative-thinking technique that uses established patterns. From these patterns, this guidebook reveals a set of power tools belonging to every creative professional's toolkit.

In this book, a "creative process" is a series of steps that lead to a big idea. Here, creative processes are divided into three subgroups: (1) creative behaviors; (2) creative techniques; and (3) creative resources. Before an individual can make full use of the techniques and resources, one must learn to become inherently creative—this can be achieved through practice. As a paradigm, this book provides a comparative look at the behavior patterns of experienced artists versus beginners, which highlights best-practice behavior patterns for pursuing big ideas. Practical techniques for ideation are described here, such as the formal brainstorming technique. Creative resources are given as well, offering big idea patterns as formulas for big ideas— similar to a chef's recipes or an architect's blueprints.

According to classic academic texts, a specific step-by-step process is involved in every instance of a big idea search. Although there is some variance in every individual's creative process, it is commonly agreed that there six stages: (1) Preparation – collecting information; (2) Frustration – working to define or solve problems, often with uneasy transitions between left and right sides of the brain; (3) Incubation – associating new and old information and arriving at new combinations; (4) Illumination – connecting two previously unrelated elements as an idea; (5) Evaluation – filtering and decision-making pertaining to the value of the idea; and (6) Elaboration – working out the execution of copy, imagery, and layout (Bendinger, 1993) (Ziegler & Johnson, 1981).

Left-Brain and Right-Brain Thinking

Daniel Pink is a bestselling author who advocates the idea that the modern workplace must evolve from "left-brained," or logical for knowledge workers, to "right-brained," or open and flexible for creative services workers. According to his book, *A Whole New Mind: Why Right-Brainers Will Rule the Future*, today's workplace has shifted from an "Information Age" to a "Conceptual Age." In Pink's perspective, the most valued degree in business is now the MFA, Master of Fine Arts. He says the MFA is the new MBA. He advocates the cultivation of six artistic "senses," to increase the likelihoods for success in today's workplace: design, story, symphony, empathy, play, and meaning (Pink, 2006). In Pink's proposed future, there is more public desire for right-brained thinking, as opposed to left-brained thinking.

The terms "divergent" and "convergent" were coined by U.S. psychologist Joy Paul Guilford in his studies of human intelligence. Guilford defined the convergent (left-brain) thought process as the ability to give the correct, logical answer to standard questions that do not require creativity, e.g. standardized multiple-choice tests. The opposite is divergent (right-brain) problem-solving: the method used to generate creative ideas by exploring a broad range of possible solutions (Salovey, Brackett, & Mayer, 2004). Tools for both divergent and convergent thinkers are given in this guidebook.

Divergent thinkers benefit most from traditional creative-thinking tools, like brainstorming, whereas the more structured, mathematical tools may be more useful to convergent thinkers (Sasser & Koslow, 2008). In divergent thinking, an individual or group uses word association, for example, making links between associated ideas to arrive at a coherent insight (Mumford, Hunter, & Byrne, 2009). Divergent thinking techniques bring people to more original solutions by priming distant concepts. Focus groups are an example of this—ideas emerge via associative thinking in an environment free of limitation, without judgment (Goldenberg, Mazursky, & Solomon, 1999). Convergent thinking techniques focus on achieving the single best answer to a challenge, emphasizing accuracy and logic. Both divergent and convergent thinkers can be successful as creative professionals, and the advertising profession is one that celebrates a balance of both types of thought processes.

------------✂--

Key Takeaways in Defining the Creative Process

- By definition, a creative process is a course of action that leads to big ideas.
- Three subgroups of creative processes are: behaviors, techniques, and resources.
- While some creative professionals favor left-brain or right-brain thought processes, the advertising profession celebrates a balance of both: creativity and logic.
- Ideation begins with preparation and ends with elaboration.
- Bestselling author, Daniel Pink, identifies six artistic senses for creative professionals to cultivate: design, story, symphony, empathy, play, and meaning.

CHAPTER 4
CREATIVE PROFESSIONALS SHOWCASE

"Building a creative dream life is not just about achieving, succeeding, or 'meeting goals.' It is also about floundering, stumbling, tripping and failing." —S.A.R.K.

"You can't use up creativity. The more you use, the more you have." —Maya Angelou

A few of the research references previously mentioned propose that the future workplace will hold high demand for creative thinking (Pink, 2006) (Florida, 2012). This idea is supported by the US Bureau of Labor Statistics' job outlook for 2010-2020. A few of the creative jobs with the highest projected rate of change include: (1) event planners, with 44% growth; (2) software developers, 30%; and (3) public relations managers and specialists, 21%. The outlook also projects growth in art-focused fields such as advertising, graphic design, interior design, and graphic design; as well as other occupations with room for creativity such as event planning, health coaching, and preschool teaching (Bureau of Labor Statistics, 2010). Assuming these predictions are correct, the future looks beautiful for creative professionals.

Celebrating the dawn of the Creative Age, or the Conceptual Age—whichever you prefer—this section of the book showcases an emerging class of creative professionals. Their stories range from free-thinker to caregiver, from paint slinger to lemonade connoisseur, and from idea farmer to bowtie aficionado. They are ordinary people with humble beginnings and grand aspirations, discovering big ideas and running with them. Their stories illustrate the range of occupations where creativity exists, making it apparent that nearly every workplace in America has a creative component. It is clear that nearly every person is capable of putting their big ideas into action.

Each of the creative professionals showcased here pushes the boundaries of creative thinking and problem solving, and in the opinion of this author, they are visionaries, leading efforts to inspire others to live creative lives and helping to make the world a better place, one big idea at a time. The spectrum of artists featured here includes eight creative roles: dream catchers, trailblazers, storytellers, designers, symphony conductors, play makers, artrepreneurs, and altruists—representing eight creative traits for all artists to find and refine in themselves. These roles are inspired by the artistic "senses" that Daniel Pink identifies as traits to cultivate for success among creative professionals, i.e. design, story, symphony, etc. (Pink, 2006). The hope of this author is that these stories reveal a common thread we all share as artists, granting us the realization that we are together in this creative spirit. Although the same spirit may at times call us to a wilderness of solitude in order to transfer its energy, the spirit connects us here and now, always, in all ways.

Eight Creative Traits to Cultivate			
Dream Catching	Trailblazing	Storytelling	Design
Symphony	Play	Artrepreneurship	Altruism

Eight creative traits are introduced and illustrated here, through the profiles of creative professionals. Artists are categorized to focus on each creative role. Individuals may choose to specialize in one area or master the spectrum.

Trait #1: ***Dream Catching*** – Witnessing the paradise in the everyday, and capturing the bliss to delight in.

David Erickson, Dream Catcher

David Erickson is a photojournalist for *Ravalli Republic* and *Missoulian* newspapers in southwestern Montana. He describes his artistic practice as follows: "Just like there are two types of solar energy—passive and active— my creative process usually takes on one of these two forms. Passive solar heating happens when sunlight strikes an object and that object absorbs the heat. My photography sometimes is like this, going into a situation with a prepared openness, ready to act quickly when something incredible strikes my eye. Active solar power is designed to maximize the sun's potential, generating electricity. When I go into a situation where I know specifically what I am looking for and have a specific idea in mind, I feel as if I am actively generating something powerful."

See DavidEricksonPhotography.blogspot.com.

Photo by David Erickson

Developing Creativity through Dream Catching

1. Being prepared to act when inspiration strikes
2. Pursuing goals directly
3. Staying open to possibilities

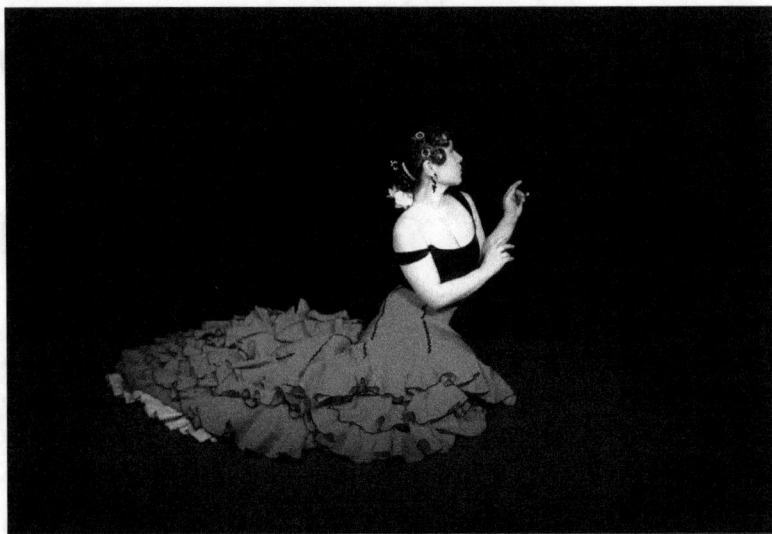

Photo by Dee Hill

Dee Hill, Dream Catcher

Dee Hill is a portrait photographer. She describes her creative inspiration as follows: "I channel my energy into the beautiful and divine aspects I see in the women I photograph. In every image there is a recollection of a story unseen from the woman's own personal life. This story is sometimes unknown to her until she sees the portrait and it speaks back information, very much like sleeping dreams carry messages to the waking sleeper. This comes from a Higher Power, and it's a gift I cherish as an artist. I work diligently to make a daily practice of the work, very much like creating chronicles in a journal about the experiences through the art of photography."

See DeeHillPhotography.com.

Developing Creativity through Dream Catching
1. Bringing forth the beauty beneath the surface
2. Making a daily practice of passionate work
3. Being in touch with a Higher Power

Dylan Hollingsworth, Dream Catcher

Dylan Hollingsworth is a documentary and archival photographer creating multimedia collections of human existence. He describes his creative inspiration as follows: "My work is best described as storytelling that focuses on our shared humanity and that offers the viewer the chance to identify with someone that there would typically be a cultural, religious or social barrier between. Through focusing on our commonalities I seek to break down the walls that exist between us as human beings and create a more human narrative of the people on the other sides of those walls— especially the marginalized, the feared and the seemingly unlovable. I also seek to show through history and present day stories what these walls can become, if not acknowledged and removed."

See DylanHollingsworth.com.

Photo by Dylan Hollingsworth

Developing Creativity through Dream Catching

1. Revealing what is imagined and making it real

2. Breaking down walls between people

3. Granting the audience access across barriers

Alan O'Hashi, Dream Catcher

Alan O'Hashi is the executive director of Boulder Community Media, as well as being a filmmaker, photographer, and board member of the Boulder International Film Festival. He describes his creative path as follows: "I've had a 30-year career using left- and right-brain approaches to problem solving—organizations today are seeing the importance of full brained thinking. Having also been a Suzuki violin teacher for a number of years, I'm truly convinced that everyone has ability to do whatever they choose—it's just a matter of using an asset or strength-based approach to developing ability. So, after being laid off a job and told to do something I always wanted to do, I dusted off my creative portfolio and decided to take pictures and write screenplays. That led to volunteering at the local public access TV station where I learned videography and editing. I eventually managed the station. Since that time I've used my public administration skills to build video production nonprofit business that produces movies and film festivals."

See BoulderCoMedia.com.

Alan O'Hashi and Boulder Community Media | Photo by Peter Wayne, PeterWaynePhotography.com

Developing Creativity through Dream Catching

1. Trusting in the potential to do whatever is desired
2. Developing ability by focusing on strengths
3. Using both left- and right-brain approaches

Trait #2: *Trailblazing* – Finding purpose, and taking the journey led by heart and free-thinking.

Isaac Clay, Trailblazer

Isaac Clay is an entrepreneur focused on community building, raw foodism, and superfoods, founding and running a co-op and superfood stores. He describes his big idea as follows: "Many ideas come, and many ideas go, as I wander around my earthly home, immersed in my daily flow. Which thoughts to choose? I must confess: it is none of these, for they are but tests. I find true inspiration in wilderness meditation. This process consists of one step for me: climb a mountain, or jump in the sea. Here I always find, big ideas come to mind; they set my spirit on fire, and in them I am inspired. My big idea received thence is thus: Master-planned garden communities where Nature is the focus, in order to create for ourselves and our posterity a Divine locus. These will be communities with the convenience of the city, the heart of the suburbs, each family with a self-sustaining forest garden, set in Nature so pristine."

Photo by Isaac Clay

Developing Creativity through Trailblazing

1. Channeling the subconscious

2. Finding inspiration in the outdoors

3. Receiving visions via meditation

Quinn Eaker, Trailblazer

Quinn Eaker is a thought leader in farming, sustainability, and health consciousness. He describes his big idea as follows: "I am here on this earth to activate a whole New Paradigm ~ a paradigm of which the experience is enjoyable ease overflowing from abundance ~;~ I am sharing this with the world very practically in the creation of New Paradigm Eco Villages and the Golden Life Program. The NP Eco Villages are living, breathing examples of how easy life is when conscious beings come together in love and common purpose. The Golden Life Program is designed to activate the awareness and ability to thrive in the most critical areas of being alive on this earth in a very practical, available and applicable way for anyone ∞§∞"

Quinn Eaker | Photo by Shellie Smith

Developing Creativity through Trailblazing

1. Building awareness of new ways of being

2. Consciously shaping the surroundings

3. Working together, with a common purpose

Joan Sheski, Trailblazer

Joan Sheski is a watercolorist and beekeeper in Grants, New Mexico. She describes her creative process as follows: "To paint anything, I try to let the flower or mountain or tree or face come in through my eyes into my heart, and from there guide my hand on the paper. There is a shared fragility about it that demands intimate attention. It is an act of love." Sheski reveals the origin point of her big ideas as follows: "There is an inner universe we all share that corresponds with its own intentions to our outer universe. We can access this universe through dreams or receptive meditation, or even by listening and seeing into, for example, the heart of a tree, animal, or person. I have come to trust this inner universe much more than the surface world I inhabit. As a watercolor artist, the inspiration for many paintings, and indeed the surprising images that emerge within the paintings I have consciously constructed, come from this world."

See PureWatercolors.com.

Joan Sheski | Photo by Cabe Lindsay

Developing Creativity through Trailblazing

1. Allowing the heart to guide the hand

2. Accessing and trusting the inner universe

3. Offering intimate attention

Vanessa Zamora, Trailblazer

Vanessa Zamora is a foodie and farmer, as well as being the founding artist behind Life That Inspires, the umbrella under which she aspires to remain fearlessly in pursuit of leading and encouraging others to live an inspirational life. She describes her big idea as follows: "I started with a near empty canvas of 17.6 acres of land and a vision to create projects that celebrate life, the creative process, community, and family. Currently in production at Lake Forest Farm is traditional and aquaponically-grown produce utilizing organic standards, a farm stand executed from a repurposed shipping container, a 1969 Prowler trailer that I'm currently renovating to become a mobile juice bar, and an event center in the early stages of development that will also be made mostly of repurposed materials and used for just about any event, but personally I will be teaching yoga and promoting it for use by other wellness professionals in the area. We also execute seasonal farm-to-table dinners featuring a guest chef, 24 dinner guests, and a seasonal four-course menu made almost exclusively from local produce and product from ours and other area farmers."

See LifeThatInspires.com and LakeForestFarm.com.

Artwork by Vanessa Zamora

Developing Creativity through Trailblazing

1. Transforming the surroundings into resources
2. Cultivating community
3. Celebrating passions

Trait #3: *Storytelling* – Voicing narrative, and encouraging communities to collectively express.

CD release poster for an original music collection by Amparo Garcia-Crow | Photo by Kevin West

Amparo Garcia-Crow, Storyteller

Amparo Garcia-Crow is a playwright and educator, immersed in the performance arts. She describes her creations as follows: "Storytelling is a strong focus of mine. An example of this is a documentary I've directed, chronicling a woman and her process to become a performance artist at the age of 65. Another example is a monthly event that I host, called 'The Living Room: Storytime for Grownups.' The Living Room is a spoken word series bringing together an eclectic mix of stories around a specific theme. These story-focused activities along with the plays I write and the dance practice I facilitate are all designed to satisfy people's need for connection and creative expression. What's my story? My occupation is a combination of writing, acting, directing, and coaching. I am an interdisciplinary artist, always in one way or another 'storytelling.'"

See AmparoGarciaCrow.com.

Developing Creativity through Storytelling

1. Seeing the art in the everyday, in everyone, everywhere
2. Holding space for collective creative expression
3. Satisfying people's need for connection

Johnny Olson, Storyteller

Johnny Olson is the founder and host of Mad Swirl, a platform for creative expression, publishing and amplifying the work of poets and storytellers. He describes his creation as follows: "Mad Swirl was born to a few of us mad ones on a winter's eve in 1999 and has grown to be exactly what we hoped it would become: a global creative outlet. The grand idea was to create a supportive space open to any and all fellow mad ones out there who had poems, stories, and pictures to share. What started as a Xeroxed zine has now blossomed into a full-blown website featuring over 100 poets, dozens of short story writers, and over 25 artists from all around this beat-utiful world of ours. We also host a live, lively monthly event featuring the loco, local mad poets and musicians from our hometown of Dallas, Texas."

See MadSwirl.com.

Mad Swirl featuring Johnny Olson | Photo by Dan Rodriguez

Developing Creativity through Storytelling

1. Shining a spotlight on creative expression

2. Amplifying the art spirit

3. Broadcasting the beautiful, the bold, and the beastly

Artwork by Andy Smetanka

Andy Smetanka, Storyteller

Andy Smetanka is an animator, whose works feature paper cutouts and silhouettes on 8mm film. He describes his creative inspiration as follows: "The Super 8 camera has been on the very cusp of obsolescence for years, yet somehow manages to stay alive. I don't know who else uses it or why, but there must be others out there somewhere helping to keep it breathing. In any case, feeling one's medium to be on the verge of extinction all the time adds a certain urgency to Super 8 projects. My big shit-just-got-real moment came when Kodak announced it would shortly be discontinuing the stock I was using to make *And We Were Young* (pictured here), an animated documentary feature about Americans in World War I. Those sudden jolts and sinking feelings just go with the territory, a sort of reverse frontier now reverting to a state of pre-film wilderness. And it's a territory I have all to myself. So it's worth it to me, for many reasons, and with all its hassles and headaches, to keep using Super 8 as long as there's a single roll of film left in the world."

Developing Creativity through Storytelling

1. Finding timeless qualities in classic crafts
2. Mastering an art form through patience and practice
3. Investing energy into rallying community support

Virginia Woodruff, Storyteller

Virginia Woodruff is the founder of Great Moments in Parenting, an online community where parents discuss "the agony and the ecstasy of life with kids, judgment-free." She describes her creative inspiration as follows: "My big idea came to me in the shower, like all great ideas. I wanted to create a 'platform' from which to publish a book, but I wasn't interested in a personal blog. Then it came to me: What if I started a blog that was open to anyone, where parents could honestly admit how crazy-making it can be to raise kids? If we all shared our true stories of parenting–the agony and the ecstasy of life with kids–we could create some something akin to group therapy and find some comic relief along the way. I think I tapped into the zeitgeist feeling that parenting is very important and very exhausting in our generation."

See GreatMomentsinParenting.com.

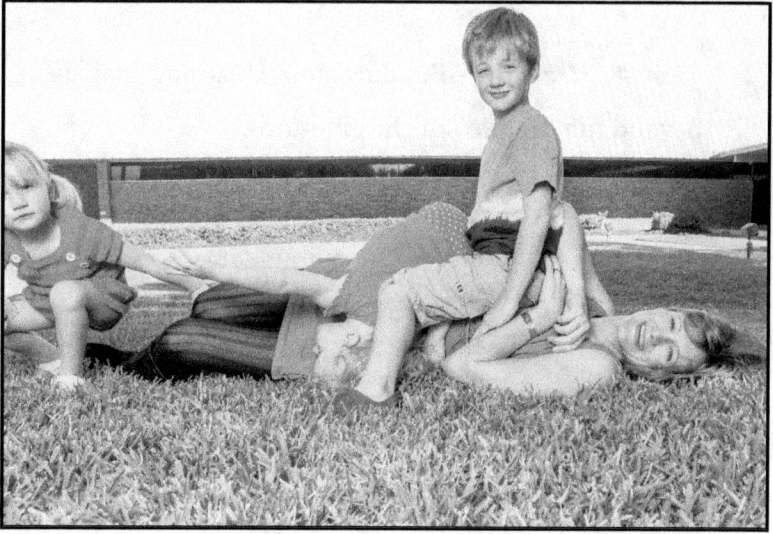

Virginia Woodruff | Photo by Annie Rey, AnnieRey.net

Developing Creativity through Storytelling

1. Engaging the audience by making experiences interactive

2. Opening the artwork for change and growth

3. Inviting collaboration, to make a big idea bigger

> Trait #4: *Design* – Building new creations that go beyond function to stir the emotions.

Lucas Aoki, Designer

Lucas Aoki is an illustrator, painter, and muralist. He describes his creative inspiration as follows: "I think we are all influenced by the world that surround us. Therefore, inspiration can come from any source. Having different interests and being passionate about other things plays, for me, a very important role in making art. Sometimes, I find new or different elements that might help me create, like another artist's work that I make a connection with, for example. Appreciating other art is a powerful source for me. Sometimes, inspiration feels random, just like a simple image that comes from within, creating new possibilities inside my head. A piece of art is an extension of me, as well as an extension of the world around me and the world inside me."

See LucasAoki.com.

Artwork by Lucas Aoki

Developing Creativity through Design

1. Appreciating the art that already exists

2. Allowing the surroundings to influence and inspire

3. Pursuing passions

Mike Johnston, Designer

Mike Johnston is an elementary art teacher and muralist, posting artwork publicly under the alias "Truth." He describes his big idea as follows: "I design street art with a positive message. My creative process starts with ideas jotted down as notes and drawings. Each idea feels brilliant when they're first sparked—but as time passes, only the strong ones keep their glow. These are the ones that I come back to and begin to create and/or collaborate with other creative souls. I try to live out a giant art project every day of my life. And sometimes the feedback from others fuels the fire, sometimes it's a desire to improve, and sometimes I can't explain why I must wake up at 4:45 am and design a street art poster meant for the public to enjoy on their commute to work. I love it!"

See MikeJohnstonArtist.com.

Artwork by Mike Johnston

Developing Creativity through Design

1. Bringing artworks to life on a daily basis

2. Practicing and improving over time

3. Receiving feedback from artists and art enthusiasts

Lane Nelson, Designer

Lane Nelson is a metalwork artist in Lander, Wyoming. He designs large scale plasma metal art like the ranch gate entrance sign shown here, measuring 20 feet long and 6½ feet tall. Nelson describes his creative process as follows: "This piece is called 'Everything Wyoming,' commissioned by a farmer who wanted to experience a Wyoming scene back at his family farm in Iowa. The challenge in metal artwork is creating a realistic setting without your ordinary art elements such as colors or shading, but with the right handling, a line itself can achieve a three-dimensional look. To gain the depth effect for this sign, I broke this scene up into three different levels: foreground, middleground, and background, with size-proportionate wildlife and trees."

Artwork by Lane Nelson | Photo by Wayne Van Wyk

Developing Creativity through Design

1. Seeing a line as more than just a line

2. Building a composition from various depths

3. Innovating in an age-old medium

Trait #5. *Symphony* – Seeing the big picture and bringing pieces together in harmony.

Monica Blossom

Monica Blossom is a community builder whose dance and music gatherings include Ecstatic cOMmUnity and Flowetry in Motion, drawing people together for elevated health, hope, and happiness. She describes her creative inspiration as follows: "Motherhood is my practice. Its rewards are beyond words and challenges. Beyond worth it. Motherhood is a Master's program in Love University. My prayer is that I give my all unconditionally, I inspire freedom, and I am kind, grateful, fierce, and graceful."

See MonicaBlossom.com.

Monica Blossom | Photo by Elizabeth Opalenik,
ElizabethOpalenik.com

Developing Creativity through Symphony

1. Achieving synergy by unifying diverse talents
2. Holding safe spaces for people to connect and express
3. Reaching out to build relationships

Caitlin Nell Lancaster, Symphony Conductor

Caitlin Nell Lancaster is a performance artist and director. She likens her creative process to this photo. "I took this picture in a neglected boat yard in Portugal and it symbolizes my approach to art. I mindfully collect ideas, memories, lessons learned, mistakes made, etc., and let them sit together, while considering what the relationships between the elements might be. Eventually, the collection of relationships settle and become something with intention; a creative piece. From an early age I was propelled by the idea of the Renaissance Woman (and Man), and as a kid I understood that anyone could follow not only a dream but many dreams, becoming masters of the arts and sciences, and living a very full life as a result. So, I drew, wrote, played music, played sports... I did it all until I became quite scattered actually! I learned to focus later, once I became a professional street performer in NYC. I adopted an improvisational approach to artistic expression through violin, dance, art and writing. Nature and ancient tradition are my deepest wells of inspiration."

Artwork by Caitlin Nell Lancaster

Developing Creativity through Symphony

1. Creating newness by combining dissimilar forms

2. Finding inspiration through nature and tradition

3. Learning focus through deep immersion

Kristina Lanuza | Photo by Suzanne Daniels Grisaffe

Kristina Lanuza, Symphony Conductor

Kristina Lanuza is an advertising executive, as well as being a Yoga teacher, singer, writer, and producer of musical theatre. She describes her creative process as follows: "I work in advertising as a Digital Project Manager, and I've found that having a creative process is highly necessary for getting something done. I'll have to say that writing a musical about Yoga is the biggest creative endeavor I've ever tackled. And the process is not something I would imitate in fast-paced advertising, nor in many other small musical gigs that I do. It's something like five years of concepting (dreaming, meandering, free-form), and finally, boom, an understanding of how the plot thickens and ends. Somehow coming up with an ending conceptually is crucial. And now I can go on about producing each piece of music, one-by-one. I'm hoping to produce 10 songs in 9 months. Like 9 months gestation before having a baby."

See Yogafly.com.

Developing Creativity through Symphony

1. Confidently undertaking large-scale endeavors
2. Being receptive to ebbs and flows of creativity
3. Enduring the ups and downs of a long-term commitment

Nathan Zavalney, Symphony Conductor

Nathan Zavalney is an audio specialist, recording artist, instructor, and director of the Childbloom Guitar Program. He describes his big idea as follows: "Through my fascination with multi-track recording, I've had a long-time love affair with creating layered musical worlds. This led me into live improvised musical accompaniment for yoga and dance in classes and performances. I wanted to have access to a giant pallet of sounds that I could use to create lush sound spaces in real time relation to the teachers and performers that I was collaborating with. So I began designing and building a musical setup that would allow me to combine sample/synthesizer technology with acoustic instruments, using interfaces and techniques that allow me to simultaneously control multiple layers of sounds; playing guitar with my right hand while playing a sampled Armenian Duduk sound mixed with an atmospheric synth sound on a keyboard with the volume being controlled by my breath, while holding a rhythm with my right foot on an amplified stomp box, and using my left foot to control various pedals to sustain and trigger sounds. It has been a frustrating, joyous, ongoing process of investing money and time into design and practice with my ever-evolving contraption of instruments and technology."

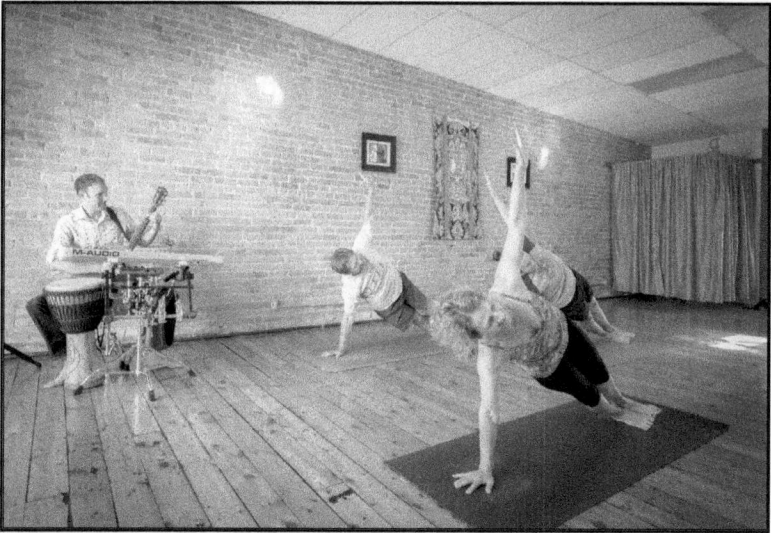

Live music featuring Nathan Zavalney

See MissoulaSoundworks.com and MissoulaChildbloom.com.

Developing Creativity through Symphony

1. Fine-tuning the tools necessary to get the job done

2. Blending layers to create something unique

3. Allowing the craft to evolve

Trait #6: *Play* – Elevating life with a pleasure and lightness that lifts others up.

BodyJuggling image featuring SaTek Ananda

SaTek Ananda, Play Maker

SaTek Ananda is the founder of BodyJuggling, an elite lifestyle fitness company based on the principles of tai chi, yoga and acrobatics. He describes his big idea and creative process as follows: "The body, mind and spirit are not separate components, merely different aspects of the same one experience. The more we unify the body, mind and spirit through movement, breath and awareness, the more effortless life becomes. In my experience, achievement comes in four steps: clarifying the purpose, practicing skills, structuring the elements, and executing the plan. For example, I grew up traveling with the Ringling Bros. Circus and learned the power of training to accomplish anything I desired by the age of six, when I taught myself to ride the unicycle."

See BodyJuggling.com.

Developing Creativity through Play

1. Clarifying the intention
2. Navigating purposefully through the action
3. Moving holistically, with body, mind, and spirit

Sebastien Gendry, Play Maker

Sebastien Gendry is the founder of Laughter Wellness, a body-mind healing methodology focused on bringing laughter and joy in the body to create overall wellness in body and mind. He describes his creative process as follows: "There is a simple way to unlock the Pandora box of unlimited ideas and break free from our own self-imposed limitations and inhibitions. In the context of what I do it means engaging in the movements of laughter, joy and empowerment—preferably in a group—to create that very chemistry for a variety of purposes. We do this by choice, and so there are no jokes or comedy. We simulate to stimulate, so we use lots enthusiasm. It can be awkward at the beginning, and it takes time to overpower the mind and shift its thinking processes from negative to positive, from stuck to flowing into a world of possibilities. This is because whenever you tie your mind to a conscious physical process, you enter the field of present moment awareness (the body cannot time travel. It always here, now.) That space is the homeland of creativity and infinite potential because it is beyond the duality of judgment. You can't define who you are and who you are not, what you can or can't do when you have no past and no future. It's both the beginning and the end, full and empty, everything and nothing."

Laughter Yoga featuring Sebastien Gendry

See LaughterWellness.org.

Developing Creativity through Play

1. Choosing the desirable attitude

2. Being present, here and now

3. Participating in community with enthusiasm

Naya Jones | Photo by Fanny Trang

Naya Jones, Play Maker

Naya Jones is the owner and facilitator of Rootwork, a series of events and classes promoting mindfulness and creative expression. She describes her creative outlets as follows: "Big ideas in my life come from my 'healthy' obsession with one central metaphor: roots. As an owner of Rootwork, I draw on my cultural roots as a Black and Mexican woman to share meditation, movement, and ceremony with diverse communities. I help folks get rooted in their lives; I help people reconnect with their bodies. As a co-founder of Food for Black Thought, these same practices help me facilitate hard conversations about food injustice. The practices I treasure are my creative process; with meditation, movement, and ceremony I stop, I pause, I receive, and I midwife the big ideas into the world."

See Root-Work.com.

Developing Creativity through Play
1. Drawing on culture and personal values for inspiration
2. Exchanging ideas among like-minded people
3. Enjoying the journey as well as the destination

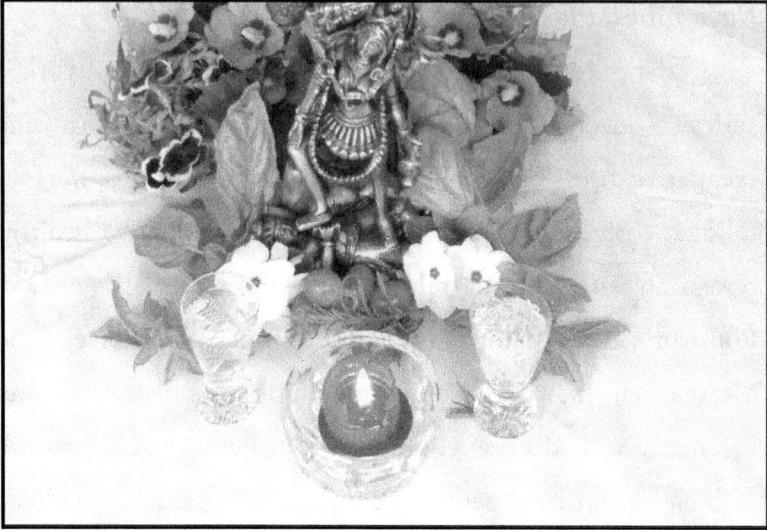

Artwork by Deb Kern

Deb Kern, Play Maker

Deb Kern, Ph.D., is a health scientist, author, and internationally acclaimed speaker on mind/body/spirit health. She describes her creative inspiration as follows: "When I do one-on-one Intuitive Guidance sessions for clients over the phone I create an altar for them before the call. In the creation process I am drawn to place certain items on the altar, which becomes key to the questions and issues they present to me. This creative process has unfolded in the most powerful (and helpful) way."

See DrDebKern.com.

Developing Creativity through Play

1. Focusing on what comes naturally
2. Making the workspace sacred
3. Heeding to alternative sources of guidance

Trait #7: *Artrepreneurship* – Organizing and presenting gifts that bring wonder into the world.

Jess Decelle, Artrepreneur

Jess Decelle is the founder of Fox & Brie, a clothing line of handcrafted menswear, specializing in bow ties, neckties & pocket squares. She describes her creative inspiration as follows: "As a child, when asked by well-meaning adults what I wanted to be when I grew up, I answered politely, 'I just want to make neat things and go on lots of adventures.' It's taken 27 years and two college degrees to realize that I just need to create useful, beautiful things for people to enjoy. As a creative entrepreneur, my happiness relies more on the intangible acts of production than on the finished product itself. I'm drawn to the intricate & timeless nature of menswear, which inspired me to launch a line of vintage-inspired men's accessories, Fox & Brie. So today I make bow ties, but tomorrow could bring an entirely new adventure."

See FoxandBrie.com.

Artwork by Jess Decelle

Developing Creativity through Artrepreneurship

1. Recognizing pleasure in the production process

2. Enhancing classics with a modern touch

3. Making the functional fantastic

Tim Scott, Artrepreneur

Tim Scott is the designer and co-founder of Mitscoots Socks, a company that matches every pair of socks purchased with an equal pair of given to a person in need. He describes his big idea as follows: "For years I have dreamed about using solid business ideas to conquer social issues around the world. Well my thought is: 'What if we could focus all our productivity into a philanthropic cause?' I would say there about a thousand different hurdles in the way of accomplishing that goal, but there is also one constant variable that keeps me moving along and making things happen—people want to be part of something bigger than themselves and know in their hearts that what they do matters. Well, I know that they are right, so I make sure that my ideas are always bigger than life and inclusive for the people that want to dream along with me. One man's great idea is revolutionary, but a great idea owned by the people is a revolution."

See Mitscoots.com.

Tim Scott

Developing Creativity through Artrepreneurship

1. Including others in living the dream
2. Having compassion for other people's living situations
3. Responding to calls for help

Mikaila Ulmer, Artrepreneur

Mikaila Ulmer is a child entrepreneur who created BeeSweet Lemonade as a 4-year-old. By her 8th birthday, her lemonade was successfully bottled and broadly (locally) marketed. She describes her big idea as follows: "My lemonade is special because it's sweetened with honey. Local honey. It also has mint and flaxseed. A lot of people say it is Bee-licious. I got the recipe from my great granny Helen's 1940s cookbook. I am passionate about saving the bees because one out of every three bites we eat are pollinated by the bees. I even donate money from the sale of BeeSweet Lemonade to organizations fighting hard to save the honey bee. So, when you buy a bottle you help save a bee. Love & Lemonade, Mikaila."

See BeeSweetLemonade.com.

Mikaila Ulmer and BeeSweet Lemonade | Photo by Sandra Ramos, SandraRamosPhoto.com

Developing Creativity through Artrepreneurship

1. Giving gifts graciously

2. Spreading the cheer

3. Remembering the little things that make life sweet

Trait #8: *Altruism* - Showing care and kindness, devoted to the wellbeing of others.

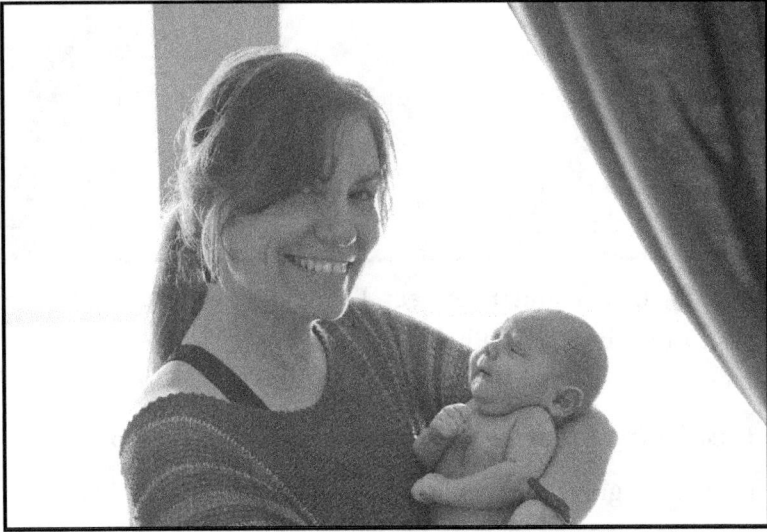

Illysa Foster | Photo by Leilani Rogers, PhotosByLei.com

Illysa Foster, Altruist

Illysa Foster, M.Ed., CPM, is a psychotherapist and midwife, providing holistic and comprehensive prenatal care, support during labor and birth, and postpartum care. She describes her big idea as follows: "Mothers and babies are intimately connected in utero and beyond. When clinicians and parents pay close attention, they can communicate with the baby before, during and immediately after the birth. As the mother progresses through the childbearing year, she and her family begin to appreciate the emerging 'mamababy,' in which mother and baby are attached physiologically, emotionally, socially and cognitively. To best meet the needs of mothers and their babies, communities and health care providers must learn to appreciate the oneness of mother and baby before, during and after the birth."

See MamaBabyTherapy.com.

Developing Creativity through Altruism

1. Listening intently and communicating tenderly
2. Attending to unspoken requests
3. Safeguarding the tendrils of connection between people

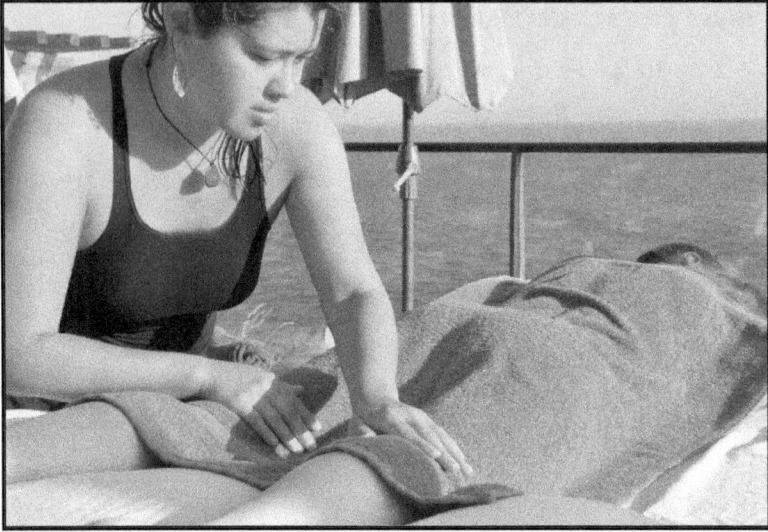

Susanne Haces at The Esalen Institute

Susanne Haces, Altruist

Susanne Haces is a massage therapist and holistic health practitioner. She describes her creative path as follows: "I am creating a whole body wellness practice that combines moving meditation with body therapy and education in nutrition. I'm especially interested working with groups including elders and young adults, finding the soft connection of embodiment with movement on and off the table is my focus. Presently, for me, it has been a six year journey moving with the 5Rhythms dance meditation, receiving certification in Esalen massage, and refining my practice of health coaching in the Integrative Nutrition method. I envision retreats fueled on high quality foods while teaching the importance of nourishing ourselves on a cellular level to free our minds and bodies into deeper movement."

See DallasHealthCoach.com.

Developing Creativity through Altruism

1. Learning and mastering skillsets that serve others
2. Advocating and exemplifying healthy decisions
3. Encouraging self-expression

Kate Short Lindsay, Altruist

Kate Short Lindsay is the creator of InnerHum, a health coaching service. She describes her big idea as follows: "I support women in transforming into the most beautiful, self-accepting, wholly healthy (in body, mind and spirit), full of life women they can be. To do this, I facilitate a women's group called 'Women Who Dance with Life,' and I lead online wellness programs: 'Feed Your Life' and 'Spring Alive Whole Life Cleanse.' I also co-created the 'Resilient Mamas' online community and wellness program for mothers. These are creative group forums, where women discuss health topics, share stories, and dive heart first into self-expression. Being witnessed in these ways allows each woman to feel she is enough, and she is supported."

See InnerHum.org and ResilientMamas.com.

Kate Short Lindsay | Photo by Holly Wilmeth,
HollyWilmeth.com

Developing Creativity through Altruism

1. Witnessing and being witnessed

2. Helping people transition through changes

3. Leading people in realizing their highest aspirations

------------✂--

Key Takeaways in the Creative Professionals Showcase

- Creative professionals are categorized into eight roles, representing distinct skillsets that can be cultivated in every artist.
- The eight traits associated with these creative roles are developed in the following ways, for starters:
  - Dream Catching: (1) being prepared to act when inspiration strikes; (2) bringing forth the beauty beneath the surface; (3) revealing what is imagined and making it real; and (4) trusting in the potential to do whatever is desired.
  - Trailblazing: (1) channeling the subconscious; (2) building awareness of new ways of being; (3) allowing the heart to guide the hand; and (4) transforming the surroundings into resources.
  - Storytelling: (1) seeing the art in the everyday, in everyone, everywhere; (2) shining a spotlight on creative expression; (3) mastering an art form through patience and practice; and (4) engaging the audience by making experiences interactive.
  - Design: (1) appreciating the art that already exists; (2) bringing artworks to life on a daily basis; and (3) seeing a line as more than just a line.
  - Symphony: (1) achieving synergy by unifying diverse talents; (2) creating newness by combining dissimilar forms; (3) confidently undertaking large-scale endeavors; and (4) fine-tuning the tools necessary to get the job done.

- o Play: (1) clarifying the intention; (2) choosing the desirable attitude; (3) drawing on culture and personal values for inspiration; and (4) focusing on what comes naturally.
- o Atrepreneurship: (1) recognizing pleasure in the production process; (2) including others in living the dream; and (3) giving gifts graciously.
- o Altruism: (1) listening intently and communicating tenderly; (2) learning and mastering skillsets that serve others; and (3) witnessing and being witnessed.

CHAPTER 5
CREATIVE BEHAVIOR PATTERNS

"The object isn't to make art, it's to be in that wonderful state which makes art inevitable." —Robert Henri

To be successful as a creative professional, an artist must be habitually, if not innately, creative. This in itself is a practice (White, 2002) (Foster, 2007). Creative breakthroughs cannot be scheduled, but creative people can practice being creative and practice being organized, prepared, and open for creative insight when it comes. On this subject, White (2002) writes:

> We don't simply need compartmentalized creative processes such as brainstorming sessions. We need to live creative lives. We need to be creative people. We need to eat, sleep, and breathe creatively. We need to become what we want to produce—fountains of innovation.

Pablo Picasso is a good example of a creative person whose creative finesse developed over time. Picasso endured a long-term, devoted practice of preparation and mastery of his medium. His early works reflected the discipline and training he received under his mentors and art academies. Through Picasso's preparation, uniqueness naturally found its expression (Loori, 2004). Picasso said, "There are painters who transform the sun into a yellow spot, but there are others who, thanks to their art and intelligence, transform a yellow spot into the sun."

Numerous writings on the subject of creativity advise us to behave as children, with a sense of wonder and awe (Foster, 2007) (Pink, 2006) (SARK, 2004) (White, 2002) (Ogilvy, 1983). Children live in the present moment and address problems by seeing situations freshly each time. They play, without getting hung up on the risks of playing. They stand up in the boat and rock it. They shout out loud in church houses and grocery stores. They pound the piano with their fists. Importantly, children employ spontaneity. "They constantly see the new relationships among seemingly unrelated things. They paint trees orange and grass purple, and they hang fire trucks from clouds" (Foster, 2007).

Children are born with the ability to fly vicariously through a kite, as seen here at the 85th Annual Zilker Kite Festival, in Austin, Texas.

In addition to behaving like children, there are two additional behavioral patterns that can help creative professionals to be more idea prone: (1) optimizing self-image; and (2) believing in success. Each of these is a mental behavior pattern that has been widely attributed to achievement in right-brain thinking. This is not merely a New Age self-help concept, like The *Power of Positive Thinking* (1952) or *The Secret* (2006), although this author finds no fault in the messages therein. The concept that the mind can alter the body is a scientifically-proven fact, e.g. seeing a scary movie makes the heart race. Human beings can alter their lives by shaping their attitudes, and because of this, it is important for artists to optimize self-image and to believe in success. Through practice, confidence can be learned.

On the subject of becoming idea prone, longtime creative director, Jack Foster, writes: "Your self-image determines what you are and how you perform." To Foster, the best way to significantly improve one's performance is to improve one's confidence (Foster, 2007). The first step in achieving self-confidence is to focus on the present moment, like a child, where a person can be free from troubles of the past or concerns about the future (Loori, 2004). Self-confidence is heightened through life experiences, e.g. letting oneself be seen and heard, while deeply expressing genuine feelings. Every experience offers the potential for inspiration and growth as a creative thinker. Creative expression such as photography, poetry, singing, and dancing are right-brain exercises that develop confidence (Barry, 2008) (Foster, 2007) (Minsky, 2007) (SARK, 2004).

Regarding general creative behaviors, professional artists advise a positive attitude. Foster writes: "If you think of yourself as successful you will probably become successful." He declares that an individual's ability to generate big ideas is wholly dependent on whether or not the individual believes he or she can generate big ideas (Foster, 2007) (Cameron,

2002). The ability to come up with big ideas begins with the belief in the existence of big ideas, which can be learned through perusing award-winning ads published in annuals, for example. Believing is achieving, as the saying goes, and so the next step in being idea prone is a belief in the self as being capable of generating big ideas. The final step is to see beyond the self as a success story of a big idea, e.g. visualizing one's recognition at an awards ceremony (Foster, 2007) (Loori, 2004).

Ironing out one's creative behaviors makes one more likely to find success in utilizing creative techniques and resources. In addition to toning creative behaviors by optimizing self-image, believing in success, and free-thinking without filtering, there are opportunities elsewhere as well. There are advantages in experiencing life even if it means breaking rules, and even if it leads to failure. In fact, great advances in the sciences and arts are the direct result of rule breaking.

"Pablo Picasso broke the rules on what a woman's face should look like. e.e. cummings broke the rules on what poems should look like. David Ogilvy broke the rules on how copywriting should sound," Foster writes. He concludes: "The only way to know that you've gone far enough is to go too far—going too far is called failing. But if you don't go far enough in searching for an idea, then you can't be sure you've got the best idea" (Foster, 2007).

Being childlike is a sign of maturity in creative processes, noticeable in one's willingness to be spontaneous, suspend disbelief, and dwell in the present moment. In fact, researchers and creative professionals agree that successful, advanced artists are more likely than beginners to express thoughts openly, free-write freely, and brainstorm uninhibited. During ideation, inexperienced artists limit themselves by filtering, and ruling out ideas, whereas advanced artists are less likely to self-edit. While beginners have perfectionist, resistant tendencies, advanced artists let go of their restraints and let the ideas flow (Griffin, 2008) (SARK, 2004).

Advanced Artists Versus Beginners

The Griffin study (2008) investigated the ideation process of creative teams, aiming to "demystify the process and make it more accessible to all." This article compared techniques employed by advanced artists versus beginners. The key technique of interest here is called "mindscribing." For advanced participants in the Griffin study, mindscribing involved a technique of writing assorted notes, spontaneously and eclectically archiving and organizing their thoughts. They emphasized the value of writing everything down, as this practice served to clear and open their minds—the act of recording a thought essentially removed it from their subconscious clutter in order to make room for new ideas. Advanced students were less likely to self-edit while doing this type of writing whereas inexperienced students limited themselves by filtering, and ruling out ideas (Griffin, 2008).

The Griffin report found strong evidence suggesting a route that enables creative professionals to develop their expertise: acquire ideation strategies and then experiment with them to determine which strategies are most comfortable and are most fruitful (Griffin, 2008). Over time, participants in the Griffin study were exposed to a wide variety of techniques, and they developed diverse, individualized toolkits of effective ideation techniques. Findings suggest that creative processes need to be customized to the person and situation at hand; the techniques are not one-size-fits-all. This tendency is revealed to be true in other studies as well, including articles by Kilgour and Koslow (2009) along with Sasser and Koslow (2008), and the book by Law (1999).

As indicated by the following diagram, techniques differ greatly between advanced participants and beginners. Chiefly, advanced participants are oriented toward the big idea whereas beginners are oriented toward the advertisement. By comparison, the technique of advanced artists is richer in resources, because of more extensive mindscribing (non-filtered) and larger collection of reliable heuristics, i.e. more tools in the toolkit, offering more possibilities. With these ample possibilities, generating a large quantity of ideas increases the likelihood of reaching quality ideas. Another notable difference is the presence of an "adaptation" phase in the advanced participants' workflows, allowing them to further develop their more viable ideas. The adaptation phase involves the generation of headlines and/or taglines related to the idea. After adaptation, the idea is considered ready to execute (Griffin, 2008).

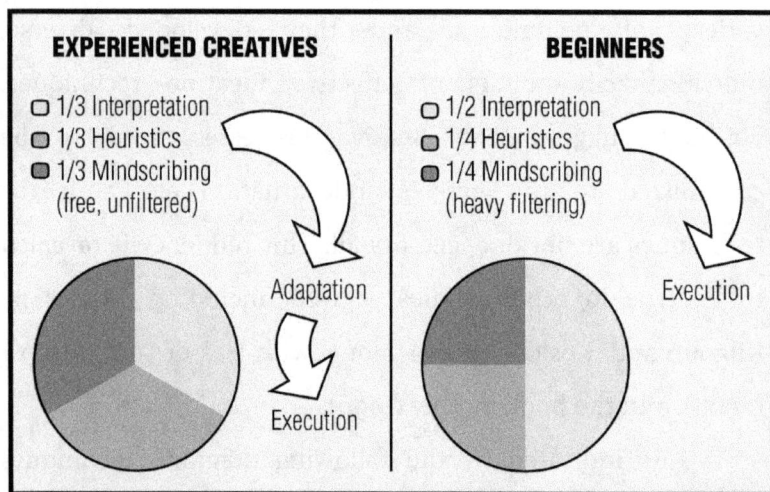

Side-by-side models comparing the creative processes of experienced artists versus beginners.

Reportedly, the ideation process of skilled artists is a two-step cycle: (1) develop an original idea; and (2) integrate the idea into a problem-solving process and generate other elaborations. According to a report by Sasser and Koslow (2008), this two-step cycle often takes less than three seconds, and will often flow quickly for seven minutes of focused attention, followed by several minutes of "rest," or reduced idea flow. The process repeats itself, and the cycle can last for hours. For beginner artists, more time is spent on elaboration. The beginners' abilities are limited, as they tend to become distracted with the tactical details of the execution (Sasser & Koslow, 2008). This behavior is also noted in the Griffin report (Griffin, 2008). The lesson here is this: cautious, apprehensive filtering is the counter-productive path of the beginner, while free-flowing, rule-breaking open-mindedness is the clear path of the advanced creative.

--------- ✂ ---

Key Takeaways in Creative Behavior

- Three behavioral patterns can help creative professionals to be more idea prone:
  - ○ Behave like children, with spontaneity and daring.
  - ○ Optimize self-image by practicing and improving.
  - ○ Believe in success, with an optimistic attitude.
- Ideation behaviors differ greatly between advanced artists and beginners.
- Beginners tend to limit themselves by filtering and ruling out ideas, distracted by the details of the execution.
- Advanced artists generate ample ideas to increase the likelihood of reaching quality ideas.
- Advanced artists include an "adaptation" phase to further develop their more viable ideas.

CHAPTER 6
CREATIVE TECHNIQUES

"The thing I hate the most about advertising is that it attracts all the bright, creative and ambitious young people, leaving us mainly with the slow and self-obsessed to become our artists." —Banksy

Why are creative thinking techniques important? Creative techniques help to direct artists through the brainstorming process in order to develop superior ideas (Kilgour & Koslow, 2009) (Goldenberg, Mazursky, & Solomon, 1999). Studies suggest that ideation techniques can simplify and improve the decision-making processes involved in designing creative strategy and execution. Creative techniques can be learned and trained as effective, efficient tools for real-life applications (Goldenberg, Mazursky, & Solomon, 1999) (Griffin, 2008).

Academics and experts have discussed some common strategies that serve as sources of inspiration. A few of their examples include: (1) Before and After – show life with or without the object; (2) Demonstration – show the object in action to dramatize its benefit; and (3) Testimonial – show people's approval of the object. Both the *Before and After* and *Demonstration* strategies are often comparative in nature, showing one object alongside another (Barry, 2008) (Bendinger, 1993). Variations on the *Testimonial* strategy include showing a spokesperson who shares positive experiences with the object, or showing the owner or staff behind the object – these techniques put viewers at ease by creating a sense of credibility, which leads to comfort and familiarity (Barry, 2008).

Along with the strategies at play in the search for big ideas, there are a variety of different idea types that serve as sources of inspiration. Idea types include: (1) King – show the subject matter's unquestionable superiority; (2) Personification – show the subject matter's influence, i.e. you are what you eat; and (3) Social Commentary – show the subject matter's presence in the rhetoric of popular culture (Barry, 2008). The *King* idea type involves messages of supreme excellence, either stated or implied. After all, an item's benefits can be exaggerated beyond truth. The *Personification* idea type may display someone using an item and then becoming that item in some way, or conversely, the item is compared to a person or human behavior. The *Social Commentary* idea type is often related to general cultural trends, movements, or current events such as global warming, all relating back to the item and its benefits.

Unbounded Randomness

The creative department of an advertising agency is responsible for ideation, illustration, copywriting, and conceiving the layout, all of which are tasks that benefit from the following type of creative process: unbounded randomness. The unbounded randomness type of creative process is a free-flowing, unfiltered mind-frame, with the goal of generating a large quantity of ideas to find surprising, innovative solutions (Tellis & Ambler, 2007). Creative processes frequently involve methods that encourage the generation of a large number of concepts on the assumption that "the best way to get a good idea is to get a lot of ideas" (Tellis & Ambler, 2007) (Goldenberg, Mazursky, & Solomon, 1999). As the number of ideas increases, there is a higher likelihood of achieving a set of quality ideas that can later be sorted, filtered, and extended (Tellis & Ambler, 2007) (Sullivan, 2008).

In any form of creative expression, ideas spring up most freely when the creator is able to work without hindrance or judgment. Keeping this in mind, criticism in art is valuable at times, but not during the ideation process (Loori, 2004). Veteran copywriter Luke Sullivan advocates writing out in simple words what is intended, to get the words flowing. Later, in Sullivan's process, he advises a fine-tuning of the message to make it memorable. His procedure is this: "First, say it straight. Then say it great" (Sullivan, 2008). Ideally, the original expression is purely creative and free-flowing, with the goal of assembling a high quantity of ideas. The *quality* of these ideas is later determined, through a process of filtering and editing, which is both creative and critical (Sullivan, 2008). Loori (2004) writes:

> In the creative process, as long as the energy is strong, the process continues. It may take minutes or hours. As long as you feel chi peaking and flowing, let it run its course. It's important to allow this flow and expression, without attempting to edit what is happening—without trying to name, judge, analyze, or understand it. The time for editing is later. The time for uninhibited flow of expression is now.

Formal Brainstorming

Brainstorming is a way of playing through the fog of a campaign by improvising, collaborating, and refining ideas. It is the most widely recognized and utilized method for creativity-enhancement (White, 2002). The formalized brainstorming technique is attributed to Alex Osborn, founder of the multinational advertising agency, BBDO. Variations exist, depending on the level of formality, etc. Basically, in brainstorming, an individual or a small group of people focuses on a problem and builds a list of words and phrases that could lead to a potential solution. The basic rule is that all ideas are worthy of inclusion. Even hollow and impractical phrases are included, as indeed, outlandish ideas often trigger constructive ones. Filtering and criticism are prohibited in brainstorm sessions because judgment stifles the flow of free-thinking (Tellis & Ambler, 2007).

In the formal method of brainstorming, there are six stages: (1) Problem – articulation and discussion of the issue at hand, e.g. apple eaters are concerned about waxed skins; (2) How-To – problem is restated and revisited as a set of purposeful objectives, e.g. how to establish a tradition of peeling the apple before consumption; (3) How Many Ways – group explores each of the objectives and lists possibilities for solving the problem, e.g. apple pie eating contest with a potato peeler giveaway; (4) Warm-Up – short session to step away from the big problem and swap ideas to get the brain muscles stretched and ready for action, e.g. naming alternative uses for an apple; (5) Free Ideation – continual flow of ideas with everything written down; (6) Wildest Idea – group considers the strangest, most illogical idea and tries to run it into something useful, e.g. Apple Bobbing Day as national holiday. The brainstorm session usually ends with an evaluative, left-brain search for quality in the quantity (Bendinger, 1993).

Formal Brainstorming Stages		
1. Problem	2. How-To	3. How Many Ways
4. Warm-Up	5. Free Ideation	6. Wildest Idea

Who says you can't schedule creativity? The formal brainstorming method has been used in the advertising profession since 1940. It is time-tested and pro-approved.

Just as the formal brainstorming technique exemplifies the unbounded randomness process, "mindscribing" and "mind mapping" do the same. Similar to brainstorming, mindscribing is a technique of writing assorted notes, impulsively and haphazardly, like a real-time transcription of one's thoughts. The mindscribing technique enables artists to build a database of raw materials—words, sketches, phrases, associations, all of which help to fuel ideation (Griffin, 2008). Mind mapping is more like a spider web of linked thoughts stemming from a central idea, resulting in the shape of a diagram that serves to generate, visualize, structure, and classify ideas and their linkages (Tellis & Ambler, 2007).

Synectics and Storyboarding

"Synectics" is a derivative of Brainstorming that calls for a precisely executed technique as a route to practical problem-solving. Specific exercises are used to stimulate fresh, rich beginning connections. These exercises include: Discontinuous Stories, Symbolic Analogies, and more. Synectics is a copyrighted technique developed by W.J.J. Gordon and George Prince, practiced by Synectics, Inc., and licensed users around the world. At its essence, synectics is a problem-solving method that stimulates thought processes of which the thinker may be unaware. This practice incorporates brainstorming and deepens it with metaphor, building a springboard for active ideas. In synectics, two or more different elements are juxtaposed to form a purposeful group. Synectics encourages the combination of distantly associated ideas from different perspectives (Tellis & Ambler, 2007) (Kilgour & Koslow, 2009).

A related technique is "storyboarding," which relies on a visual display. Not to be confused with the TV storyboard, the ideation technique by the same name is simply a visual outline of thoughts (Bendinger, 1993). For example, one could begin with a topic, e.g. applesauce is sweet. Next, the various subjects pertaining to the topic of "sweetness" are listed underneath the topic, e.g. oranges are sweet, honey is sweet, candy is sweet, etc. Candy connects with roasted marshmallows, which then connects with a campfire. In this way, applesauce connects with a campfire, and the value may be this: applesauce travel packs to be enjoyed at a campsite. From here, details pertaining to the new connection are listed underneath the respective subject: applesauce-campfire.

Morphological Matrix

In contrast to techniques that advocate unbounded randomness, there are some that call for the opposite approach: bounded regularity. Here, artists manage cognitive processes in focused, analytical sessions, as opposed to blind, illogical sessions. An example of the bounded regularity approach is the Morphological Matrix—an organized system for discovering new solutions to a specified challenge. This technique uses a grid, beginning with a column of parameters pertaining to the challenge. These parameters may include a list of pain points, a list of attributes, a list of benefits, or a list of anything else that invites further exploration. If these parameters are listed in a column, on the y-axis, then the possible solutions are listed in rows, on the x-axis.

For example, here is a challenge: Discover a new way of preparing an apple for consumption. The list of related food preparation possibilities may include: heating, cooling, blending, slicing, and mashing. Listing these five parameters in a column on the y-axis, the artist next explores various possibilities within each food preparation category. So, heating possibilities are listed to the right of "heating," and cooling possibilities are listed to the right of "cooling," and so forth. Ideas may immediately rise to the surface, e.g. steaming the apple with a melted chocolate coating, or freezing the apple with an ice cream coating. Ideally, there is an unlimited number of fields available in the rows to the right of each category, so ideation can continue until the artist is satisfied with the discovery.

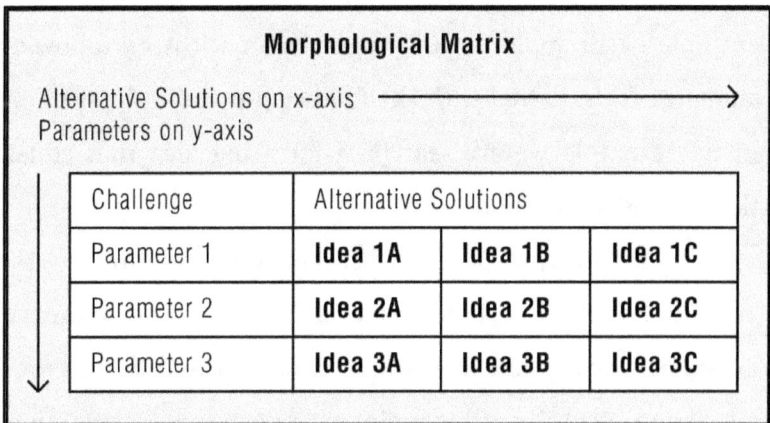

Morphological Matrix

Alternative Solutions on x-axis ————————————→
Parameters on y-axis

Challenge	Alternative Solutions		
Parameter 1	**Idea 1A**	**Idea 1B**	**Idea 1C**
Parameter 2	**Idea 2A**	**Idea 2B**	**Idea 2C**
Parameter 3	**Idea 3A**	**Idea 3B**	**Idea 3C**

The Morphological Matrix technique allows artists to approach creative challenges from a logical starting place.

Ideal for those who favor left-brain ideation techniques, grids offer a controlled structure from which to reach a comfortable chaos of creativity.

Concept Cross-Tabulation

Related to the morphological analysis is an ideation technique called, "Concept Cross-Tabulation" (CCT), by this author. This technique is sensible way of exploring a concept, useful when a creative endeavor requires a logical exploration of something abstract. Cross-tabulation can be used to morph two separate parameters of an object, such as an object's ingredients morphed with its actions, or an object's descriptive qualities with its unique selling points. A third example—one we explore here—is an object's benefits morphed with its audience. The first step in this visualization exercise is to define the audience and the benefit. In the example of an apple, a CCT might begin with the following audience: kids, paired with the following benefit: satisfaction. In this example we are searching for a big idea that equals this: apples satisfy kids.

The next step is to list concepts relating to the benefit, and then list adjectives relating to the audience, organized neatly on x- and y-axes, charted as a cross-tabulation grid. In the apple example, the "satisfaction" benefit yields the following related concepts: amazement, cheer, comfort, hope, and growth. The "kids" audience yields the following related adjectives: adventurous, curious, imaginative, energetic, and sleepy. By laying the five "satisfaction concepts" on the x-axis, with the five "kids adjectives" on the y-axis, a series of 25 fields remain open— this is where the cross-tabulation takes place. By crisscrossing concepts, one finds new associations: (1) curious growth equals an apple with a mustache; (2) adventurous comfort equals a basket of apples set on a skateboard, rolling down a hill; and (3) sleepy amazement equals apples dancing in the moonlight.

Each field in the grid reveals a new association that logically represents the given concept. Yes, the CCT technique is essentially a fill-in-the-blanks puzzle, inviting artists to think outside the box in order to solve it. The example given here uses "benefits" and "audience" as its starting point, while other CCTs may begin with alternative parameters as their starting point. New associations are expected, regardless of the starting point, as long as two sets of parameters are intelligently and imaginatively morphed.

Concept Cross-Tabulation

Equation: [Object] = [Benefit] for [Audience]
Example: Apple = Satisfaction for Kids

Benefit Concepts on x-axis ⟶
Audience Adjectives on y-axis

Benefit/Audience	Benefit A	Benefit B	Benefit C
Adjective 1	**Idea 1A**	**Idea 1B**	**Idea 1C**
Adjective 2	**Idea 2A**	**Idea 2B**	**Idea 2C**
Adjective 3	**Idea 3A**	**Idea 3B**	**Idea 3C**

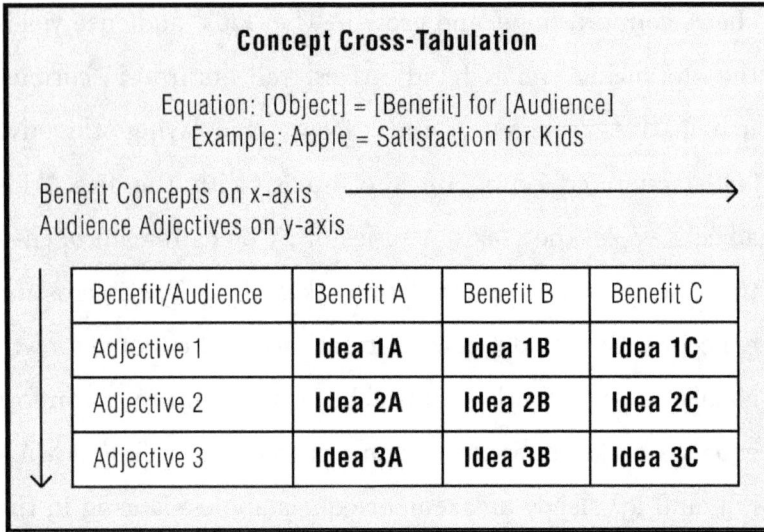

The CCT creative method is inspired by the teachings of Professor Sean Thompson, in his Art Director's Seminar course at The University of Texas.

FCB Planning Grid Explosion

The FCB Planning Grid is a technique for visualizing the audience's thoughts and feelings, thus preparing creative professionals to determine the ideal approach for reaching the audience. This technique leads to logical messaging for a target audience, in order to achieve a desired impact. This helps to keep the ideation process on-target, aligned with the artists' goals. This technique is named after Foote, Cone & Belding—the advertising agency that designed it. Here, four quadrants appear on a grid, with the X-axis revealing the audience's mind, i.e. left-brain rational ideas versus right-brain feelings. The Y-axis reveals the audience's interest level. The four quadrants of the grid are as follows: (1) high-involvement thinking, e.g. laptop; (2) high-involvement feeling, e.g. ski vacation; (3) low-involvement thinking, e.g. clothes pins; and (4) low-involvement feeling, e.g. candy bar (Bendinger, 1993).

From an advertising perspective, the FCB Planning Grid enables creative professionals to visualize the way a brand is perceived by consumers, allowing the artist to craft messaging specifically to address the consumers' perception. This is achieved by first deciding how the consumer is likely to view the brand, and second, customizing a message for this consumer in order to achieve a desired impact. Whether using the grid for advertising or some other purpose, the grid is plotted in a series of two steps: (1) plot the object in its proper coordinates on the grid; (2) plot the artistically-modified object in relation to the ordinary object (Bendinger, 1993). This technique's benefit is in visualizing the various perceptions of a given object.

To explain how the process works, let's consider an apple. An apple is a product in the low-involvement feeling category: quadrant 4, because it is essentially an easy, familiar, inexpensive product that is a satisfyingly delicious snack, for example. On the X-axis, it lies nearer the midpoint than a candy bar, since the apple is logically beneficial to one's health, making it more of a thinker's snack than a feeler's. Because the audience's perception is subjective, results may vary in the plotting coordinates and this is OK. The model holds its value even with its flexibility. Whether the apple is originally plotted in the third or fourth quadrants (step 1), an artistically-modified apple will be plotted separately (step 2), e.g. a caramel-coated apple would be plotted farther to the right. This comparison allows the creative professional to visualize one way to appeal more directly to an audience's feelings: focus on sweetness.

Once the object is plotted as a dot on the grid, a second part of this technique comes into play: "Exploding the Dot." Here, beginning with the visualization of the object in the audience's mind, ideation continues. Exploding the Dot means shifting the audience's perception 45 degrees further in any direction. This process allows artists to explore new possibilities for an object, with new insights revealed (Bendinger, 1993). For example, an apple shifted further toward low-involvement thinking might result in applesauce enriched with vitamins, packaged for school lunches. An apple shifted in the opposite direction, toward high-involvement feeling might result in a decorative wedding cake in the shape of an apple, with apple filling. In this way, new possibilities originate by visualizing the audience's perception.

FCB Planning Grid Explosion technique, with the apple plotted in quadrant 4 and then shifted 45 degrees in any direction as an exploration of various strategies for reaching the consumer's mind.

----------------✂--

Key Takeaways in Creative Techniques

- Right-brain ideation techniques employ "unbounded randomness." This is a free-flowing, unfiltered mind-frame with the goal of generating a large number of ideas.
- The formal brainstorming method is a six-step process in listing words and phrases that can lead to solutions.
- In synectics and storyboarding techniques, big ideas are found by linking of distantly associated subjects.
- Left-brain ideation techniques enable to discover new associations through logical processes.
- Concept cross-tabulation is a visualization matrix that results in new associations.
- The "FCB Planning Grid Explosion" is a technique for considering the audience's perception, thus leading to logical messaging for the audience.

CHAPTER 7
CREATIVE RESOURCES

"The whole difference between construction and creation is this: that a thing constructed can only be loved after it is constructed; but a thing created is loved before it exists."

—Charles Dickens

Like cooks with their recipe books, some artists use manuals and other tools as launching pads for ideas. There are numerous resources available to creative professionals, including "The Kickstart Catalogue," found in Mario Pricken's book: *Creative Advertising: Ideas and Techniques from the World's Best Campaigns*. The Kickstart Catalogue contains a list of approaches commonly used by artists in order to attack challenges, seeking big ideas. For example, "Comparative Juxtaposition," invites a before-and-after comparison to underscore a product benefit (Pricken, 2008). Manuals like this one belong in a creative person's toolkit, much like recipes for cooking up big ideas.

"Creativity template" is the term used by Goldenberg et al. (2009) to identify a strategic platform for uncovering big ideas, like The Kickstart Catalogue mentioned previously. Basically, a creativity template is a blueprint plan, or pattern, for acquiring big ideas. Used by creative professionals, patterns help guide the ideation process, as a sort of catapult for big ideas. The six big idea patterns identified by Goldenberg et al. are as follows: (1) Pictorial Analogy; (2) Extreme Situation; (3) Consequences; (4) Competition; (5) Interactive Experiment; and (6) Dimensionality Alteration (Goldenberg, Mazursky, & Solomon, 1999).

Yes, the Goldenberg, Mazursky, and Solomon report is a standout investigation on creative processes. This study reveals consistent patterns that underlie the world's most remarkable advertisements. In studying these award-winning ads, Goldenberg et al. identifies commonalities in the way creative professionals arrive at big ideas. Findings indicate that these "creativity templates," herein referred to as "big idea patterns," lead to effective outcomes by modeling productive creativity (Goldenberg, Mazursky, & Solomon, 1999).

The Goldenberg study defines specific patterns in the big ideas behind award-winning ads. In the Goldenberg report, some of these patterns are illustrated as diagrams, expressing the root formula. However, the diagrams are presented in a way that merely describes the commonly existing big idea patterns, as opposed to also facilitating explorations of new big ideas. With this in mind, Goldenberg's big idea patterns can be enhanced by re-engineering the logic and expressing them as fill-in-the-blank equations. To use these diagrams as creative resources, one can apply the same logic of the six classic big idea patterns into new campaigns. One can start with the underlying model, and then essentially paint by numbers to create a new ad for a new campaign.

The proposed process of using Goldenberg's big idea patterns as creative resources would involve a recycling of old patterns to arrive at new big ideas. Thus, big idea patterns can be viewed as resources that can help spur big ideas, which is in fact supported by Goldenberg et al. In theory, any object could be methodically examined, searching for big ideas with any of the six patterns. For example, let us consider an item and its respective benefit: an apple provides nourishment. Here, the product, an apple, equals the adjective, "healthy." This message, "apple equals healthy," can be plugged into one or more appropriate pattern(s), like using a scientific formula, resulting in a big idea.

Although the Goldenberg study suggests the possibility of using patterns as a resource to prompt new ideas, there is no elaboration, and no method proposed in that report; the method is proposed here for the first time. The basic step-by-step process is as follows: (1) list the object's states of being; (2) list the object's benefits; and (3) link states with benefits to arrive at new discoveries. In the first step, the word "states of being," refers to situations with respect to circumstances, i.e. conditions. For example, if the object is an apple, then the list of an apple's states of being may include: growing on a tree, being sliced, being eaten as applesauce, etc. While the first step applies to all of the six big idea patterns, the second step is specific to its particular pattern, because each of the big idea patterns explores a particular feature of the object's benefits, i.e. metaphor, result, etc.

Big Idea Pattern Process

1. List the object's states of being, i.e. descriptions, characteristics, and conditions.
2. List the object's benefits, i.e. advantages.
3. Find associations between the object's states of being and its benefits.

Big Idea Patterns					
BIP 1: Metaphor	BIP 2: Extreme Situation	BIP 3: Results	BIP 4: Competition	BIP 5: Interactive Experiment	BIP 6: Dimension Alteration
Replacement I Extreme	Alternative I Value I Attribute	Extreme I Inverted	Alternative I Value I Attribute	Activation I Imaginary	Multiplication I Division I Time Leap I New Parameter Connection

Diagram outlining the six Big Idea Patterns (BIPs) and their variations. These creative resources are reverse-engineered from the six "creativity templates" identified by Goldenberg et al. (1999), which explain the conceptual bases for 89% of 200 highly evaluated ads. Here, the templates become patterns for discovering big ideas.

Introduction to Big Idea Patterns

The testing of big idea patterns as creative resources is one that requires experimentation for substantiation. The potential value in using these tools is validated here through multiple investigative trials, including an overarching hypothetical campaign for apples as well as real-world examples of tangible objects. These illustrations are derived here, originally, by this author in order to test the worth of

Goldenberg's six identified patterns. This author's cases in point indicate the usefulness of BIPs as tools for helping artists to discover big ideas for advertising campaigns.

The Goldenberg study is based on an assessment of 500 award-winning ads and contest finalists, i.e. The One Show awards program for branded entertainment, deemed "highly evaluated" by experienced creative professionals. Of these highly evaluated ads, 89% adhered to one of the six big idea patterns (Goldenberg, Mazursky, & Solomon, 1999). To creative professionals, this study by Goldenberg et al. shows empirically that adopting these six distinct patterns can help them to generate new ideas of high quality. These big idea patterns are based on time-tested, universally powerful methods of communication that can be widely applied toward any target audiences, across products or services (Goldenberg, Mazursky, & Solomon, 1999). The use of patterns assures superior creative efforts because it facilitates a focused cognitive effort (Tellis & Ambler, 2007).

In addition to identifying the patterns present in highly evaluated ads, the Goldenberg report also found that patterns were not present in non-winning ads. The proportion of big idea patterns differs dramatically, ranging from 89% in the highest quality ads to a mere 2.5% in the non-winning ads. Among the award-winning ads that adhered to big idea patterns, the most abundant pattern is the Metaphor, or "Pictorial Analogy," accounting for 38% of the pattern-matching ads, followed by the Results, or "Consequences," pattern, accounting for 21% (Goldenberg, Mazursky, & Solomon, 1999).

------------✂--

Key Takeaways in Creative Resources

- Six consistent patterns exist in the big ideas behind award-winning ads.
- These patterns can be expressed as equations in which an artist can essentially follow the formula to arrive at big ideas.
- The 3-part process in using a big idea pattern is outlined as follows:
  - o List the object's states of being, i.e. descriptions, characteristics, and conditions.
  - o List the object's benefits, i.e. advantages.
  - o Find associations between the object's states of being and its benefits.

CHAPTER 8
BIG IDEA PATTERNS

"If you want to build a ship, don't drum up people to collect wood and don't assign them tasks and work, but rather teach them to long for the endless immensity of the sea."

—Antoine De Saint Exupery

Metaphor

The most widely used example of a pattern identified in Goldenberg's study is the *Pictorial Analogy*, here called *Metaphor*, in which a figurative symbol is introduced as a substitute for the key subject matter in an advertisement (Goldenberg, Mazursky, & Solomon, 1999). The Metaphor equation can be formulated as follows: State of Being (S) ± Metaphor (M) = Discovery (D), where variable States of Being (S_n) are linked with variable Metaphors of Benefits (M_n) to arrive at new Discoveries (D_n). Here the lowercase "n" stands for the number, so a set of three variable product conditions would be abbreviated as B1, B2, and B3, for example. Viewed as an equation, BIP 1 looks like this: Sn ± Mn = Big Idea.

Big Idea Pattern Process Example

- List the states of being (S), i.e. descriptions, characteristics, and conditions:
  o S1. apples grow on trees in orchards
  o S2. apples are stacked on display in grocery store produce aisles
  o S3. apples are eaten as snacks...
- List metaphors (M) of the benefits:
  o M1. medicine (symbol of wellness)
  o M2. a smiling heart shape (symbol of health)
  o M3. a runner's shoe (symbol of fitness)...
- Find associations (A) between the conditions ± metaphors of the benefits:
  o A1. an apple tree with smiling heart shapes replacing the apples
  o A2. an apple stuffed in a runner's shoe
  o A3. apples given as medicine over the counter by a pharmacist...

There are two variations within the metaphor big idea pattern: *Replacement* and *Extreme*. The Replacement version is illustrated in the example of an apple tree with smiling heart shapes replacing the apples—the symbol replaces the product. The Extreme version adheres to the same formula, except the concept features a symbol taken to the extreme (Goldenberg, Mazursky, & Solomon, 1999). An Extreme Metaphor pattern might portray jumbo-size medicine jars containing apples given by pharmacists as prescribed by doctors—the symbol is exaggerated to the extreme.

Two tangible brand campaigns are provided here to further illustrate BIP 1. In the Billabong wetsuit campaign, the list of variable States of Being (Sn) includes: (S1) water surface sports like surfing; (S2) underwater sports like scuba diving; (S3) offbeat sports like shark wrestling or jellyfish riding... The list of variable Metaphors of Benefits (Mn) include: (M1) a blanket (symbol of warmth); (M2) (symbol of comfort); (M3) (symbol of protection)... Metaphors of Benefits (Mn) combined with States of Being (Sn) result in Discoveries (Dn) like this: a baby asleep in a crib with a wetsuit replacing a blanket.

The second illustration of BIP 1 is a brand campaign for NASA. Here, the list of variable States of Being (Sn) includes: (S1) outer space exploration; (S2) flying vehicles; (S3) scientific discovery... The list of variable Metaphors of Benefits (Mn) include: (M1) a telescope (symbol of discovery); (M2) a rocket (symbol of flight); (M3) a planet (symbol of exploration). Sn ± Mn = a seagull replacing a man, wearing an astronaut helmet in deep space.

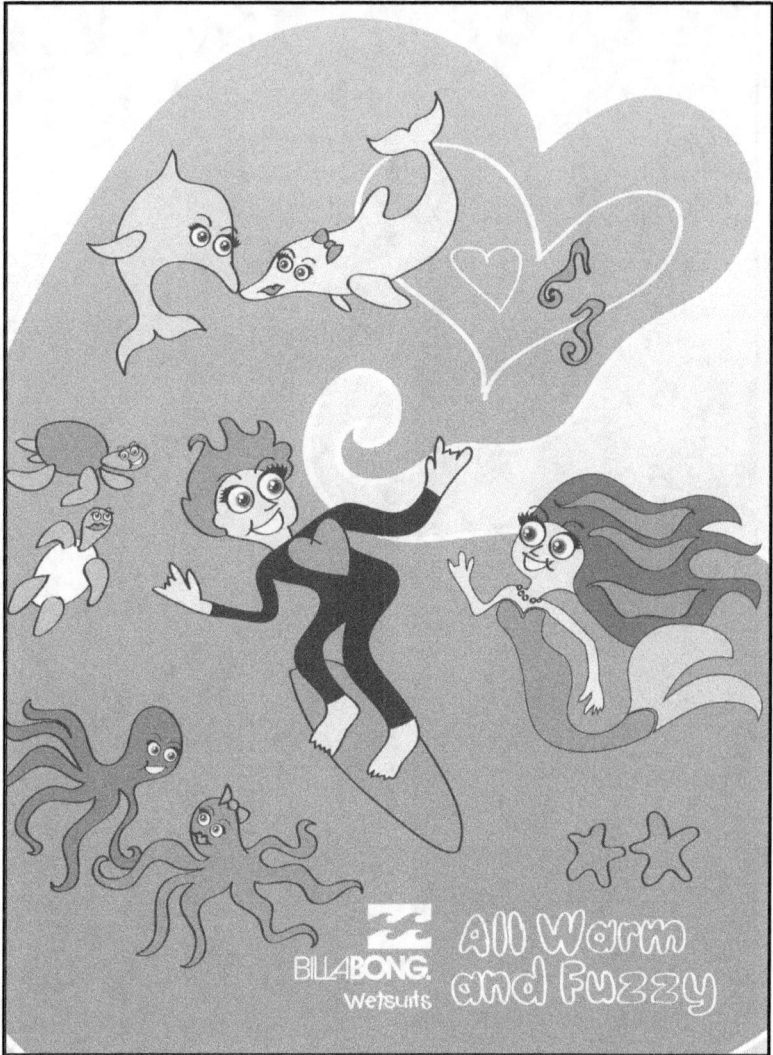

Metaphor Example 1 | Billabong wetsuits - "All Warm and Fuzzy." The brand's comfort benefit is sensationalized in this example of the Extreme Metaphor variation of BIP 1.

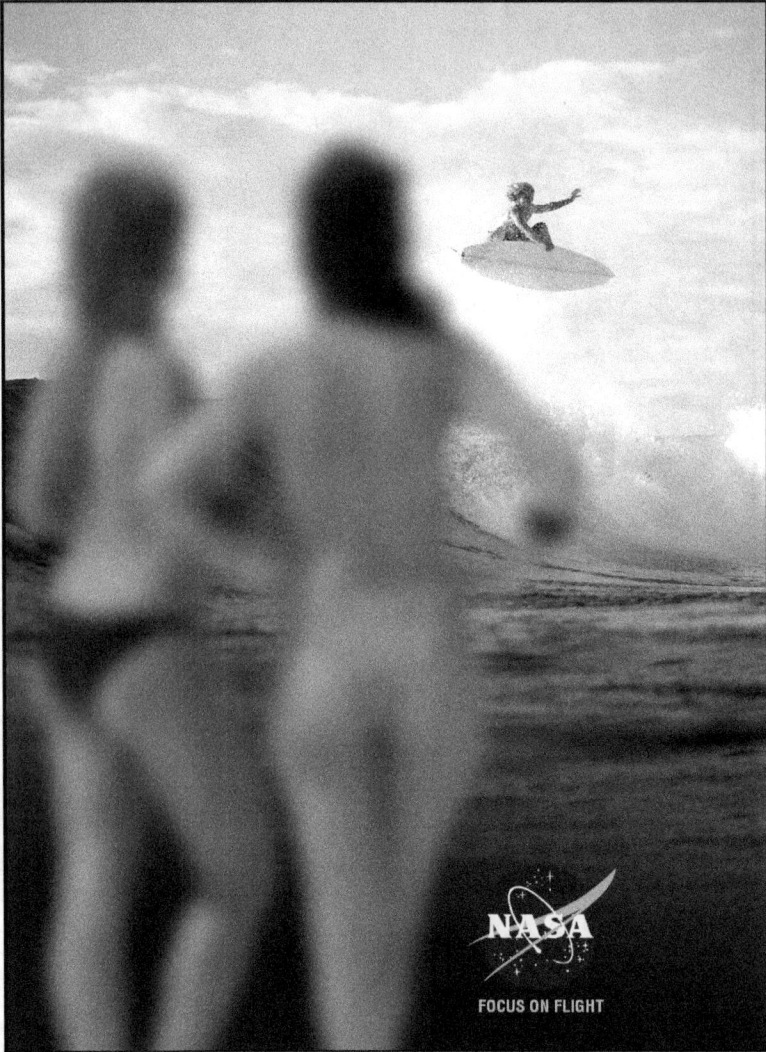

Metaphor Example 2 | NASA quantum machines - "Focus On Flight." This Extreme Metaphor variation of BIP 1 links a flying vehicle with an exaggerated symbol of discovery: focused vision.

Extreme Situation

The second big idea pattern is the *Extreme Situation*. Here, the word, "extreme," refers to uncommon, absurd, surprising, and otherwise exaggerated situations. With this pattern, unrealistic situations enhance the prominence of key attributes in a product or service (Goldenberg, Mazursky, & Solomon, 1999). Using the example of the apple again, some of the attributes include: healthy, juicy, and vitamin-rich; all qualities that can be exaggerated. The apple attribute, "healthy," is comparable to the benefit presented by variable options, such as oranges and other fruits, obviously, and more absurdly, a vitamin sandwich: a heap of various pills placed on a hamburger bun. The extreme situation equation can be formulated as such: State of Being (S) ± Extremity of Benefit (E) = Discovery (D), where variable States of Being (Sn) are linked with variable Extreme Conditions (En) to arrive at new Discoveries (Dn). As an equation, BIP 2 looks like this: Sn ± En = Big Idea.

There are three variations in the extreme situation pattern: *Alternative*, *Value*, and *Attribute*. In all of these examples, the qualities of an object are exaggerated to unrealistic proportions (Goldenberg, Mazursky, & Solomon, 1999). The Alternative form of the Extreme Situation pattern shows the value of an object by introducing an absurd alternative. For example, in a world without fibrous fruits and vegetables, restaurant side dishes might include tree bark, blades of grass, and leaves. The Value and Attribute variations of the Extreme Situation pattern each exaggerate the qualities and worth of the object in order to enunciate its benefits. An example of an exaggerated value is this: Sir Isaac Newton sitting under an apple tree, when an entire branch falls and lands on his head. An example of an exaggerated attribute is this: a blind apple farmer takes a big bite out of a dirt clod, when he mistakes it for a fallen apple.

Two tangible brand campaigns are provided here to further illustrate BIP 2. The first example is a campaign for City Harvest, an organization that "rescues" food for the hungry. The list of variable States of Being (Sn) includes: (S1) soup kitchens; (S2) food preparation; (S3) food delivery... The list of variable Extremes of Benefits (En) include: (E1) death from hunger and rebirth as a grasshopper (absurd alternative); (E2) homeless people well-fed and dancing merrily (extreme value); (E3) dining in utmost elegance and refinement (extreme quality)... Sn ± En = a royal family dining side-by-side with homeless people at a soup kitchen's community table.

The second illustration of BIP 2 is a brand campaign for Rip Curl surfboards. Here, the list of variable States of Being (Sn) includes: (S1) ocean shoreline crowded with surfers; (S2) surfboards on car racks; (S3) people sunning at the beach... The list of variable Extremes of Benefits (En) include: (E1) surfing down an escalator at a shopping mall (absurd alternative); (E2) a compact surfing treadmill for the livingroom (extreme value); (E3) a sea with colossal waves (extreme quality)... Sn ± En = a lone bicyclist on a country road with a huge surfboard mounted to the bicycle, heading to a private beach.

Extreme Situation Example 1 | City Harvest outreach program - "Food Doesn't Fall from the Sky." This example of the Value variation of BIP 2 links the hunger challenge with an exaggerated solution: food falling from the sky.

Extreme Situation Example 2 | Rip Curl surfboards - "One Man's Disaster is Another Man's Dream." This example of the Attribute variation of BIP 2 links the problem of crowded surf spots with an exaggerated solution: colossal waves.

Results

The next big idea pattern, *Results*, emphasizes the effects of either executing or failing to execute the recommendations supported in the message. Here, the word "results" is a replacement for the Goldenberg term, "consequences"—this distinction changes the negative tonality of a "penalty" to the neutral tone of an "effect" for one's action or inaction, which could be either favorable or unfavorable. Two variations are named in the Goldenberg report: *Extreme* and *Inverted*. The difference in the two variations is this: the Extreme variation implies extreme results for executing the ad's recommended course of action, while the Inverted variation implies results for not executing the ad's recommendation (Goldenberg, Mazursky, & Solomon, 1999). The formula for the Extreme Situation equation is this: State of Being (S) ± Results of Benefit (R) = Discovery (D), where variable States of Being (Sn) are linked with variable Results (Rn) to arrive at new Discoveries (Dn). Viewed as an equation, BIP 3 is: Sn ± Rn = Big Idea.

Examples of both Extreme Results and Inverted Results patterns are given here. In the consumption of an apple, results include: doctors run out of business because the apples eaten each day are keeping them away; and Adam and Eve have to learn to crochet clothing to hide their nakedness. Doctors out of work and nudists needing clothing are two extreme results (Rn) of apple consumption. Juxtaposing one of the Rn possibilities with a variable state of being (Sn), like an apple farm, the following association is born: a group of doctors rioting on an apple orchard with signs vilifying the consumption of apples, e.g. "Johnny Appleseed is a Socialist." Conversely, a few results of non-consumption include: enormous weight gain; apple farmers out of business; and the disappearance of the Johnny Appleseed legacy. Inverted results could be depicted by a screenshot of a Wikipedia search page, with "Johnny Appleseed" typed in the search engine and the resulting: "No Results Found."

To illustrate the use of BIP 3 further, let us consider two tangible brand campaigns. First is a campaign for Motorola Talkabout two-way radios, a.k.a. walkie-talkies. The list of variable States of Being (Sn) include any occasion for communication in a rural environment, especially outdoor adventures in rural areas: (S1) hunting and fishing; (S2) dog sled racing; (S3) boating... The list of variable Results of Benefits (Rn) include: (R1) backpackers miles apart can find each other (extreme result); (R2) two boats get tangled when they cross each other's fishing lines (inverted result); (R3) a Boy Scout gets lost in the woods at night (inverted result)... Results of Benefits (Rn) combined with States of Being (Sn) result in Discoveries (Dn) like this: Mrs. Claus contacts Santa moments before his sled departs on Christmas Eve, letting him know he's forgotten his bag of toys.

The second illustration of BIP 3 is a brand campaign for REI. Here, the list of variable States of Being (Sn) includes: (S1) camping gear; (S2) wilderness survival tools; (S3) ski equipment... The list of variable Results of Benefits (Rn) include: (R1) people have close encounters with wildlife (extreme result); (R2) people camp cozily in a severe rainstorm (extreme result); (R3) a caveman is found frozen in ice (inverted result)... Sn ± Rn = the lone survivor of an Ice Age apocalypse is a person bundled through the night in an REI sleeping bag.

Results Example 1 | Motorola Talkabout two-way radios - "In Touch in the Outskirts." This Extreme Results variation of BIP 3 features a woman holding the mask of Zorro, who's left it behind. Her effort to save him exaggerates the positive results of using the brand.

Results Example 2 | REI recreational equipment - "When Nature Calls You Wild." An elk looks up and sees a skier approaching the edge of a steep cliff in this example of the Extreme Results variation of BIP 3.

Competition

The *Competition* big idea pattern portrays situations in which the object competes with another product or service. The selection of the other product or event is guided by its expected superiority over the advertised object. Variations here are similar to those in the Extreme Situation pattern: *Alternative, Value,* and *Attribute,* except in this case the focus is on the competition between one product and another. Also similar to the Extreme Situation BIP, the particular conditions being compared here are generally sensationalized (Goldenberg, Mazursky, & Solomon, 1999). The formula here is: State of Being (S) ± Competitive Benefit (C) = Discovery (D), where variable States of Being (Sn) are linked with variable Competitive Benefits (Cn) to arrive at new Discoveries (Dn). The BIP 4 equation is written as follows: Sn ± Cn = Big Idea.

The Alternative form of the Competition pattern shows the value of an object by introducing an absurd alternative. For example, an apple is superior to a pine cone when used as bait for trapping a wild boar, and the same is true when used as a tool for knocking down a frisbee from a tree. The Value and Attribute variations of the Competition pattern each exaggerate the qualities and worth of the object in order to enunciate its benefits. An example of an exaggerated value is this: by comparison, an apple is more valuable than a stack of '100 bills to a dehydrated desert animal. An example of an exaggerated attribute is this: by comparison, an apple is safer than a bowl of soup while eaten by the driver of a moving vehicle.

Two tangible brand campaigns are provided here to further illustrate BIP 4. The first example is a campaign for Jackson Hole Mountain Resort, a recreational destination in Wyoming. The list of variable States of Being (Sn) includes: (S1) horseback riding; (S2) rock climbing and ice climbing; (S3) skiing and snowboarding... The list of variable Competitive Benefits (Cn) include: (C1) safer and more accessible than the moon for casual mountain climbs (absurd alternative); (C2) seeing wildlife in the wild instead of in cages at a zoo (extreme value); (C3) prefered by honeymooners as a romantic getaway, unlike a crowded amusement park like Disneyland (extreme quality)... Sn ± Cn = two overweight people riding on the back of a single zebra standing still inside a small cage.

The second illustration of BIP 2 is a brand campaign for Moto Guzzi motorcycles. Here, the list of variable States of Being (S_n) includes: (S_1) open roads; (S_2) riding tandem with a spouse; (S_3) wearing leather... The list of variable Competitive Benefits (C_n) include: (C_1) more flexibility than driving the Oscar Mayer Weinermobile (absurd alternative); (C_2) drives coast-to-coast significantly faster than a skateboard (extreme value); (C_3) tandem riding is more intimate on a motorcycle, compared to a bicycle (extreme quality)... $S_n \pm C_n$ = a motorcycle standing at the top of a grassy hillside, with a trail of two people's clothing leading out of the frame. shoes, shirt, dress, pants, underwear..

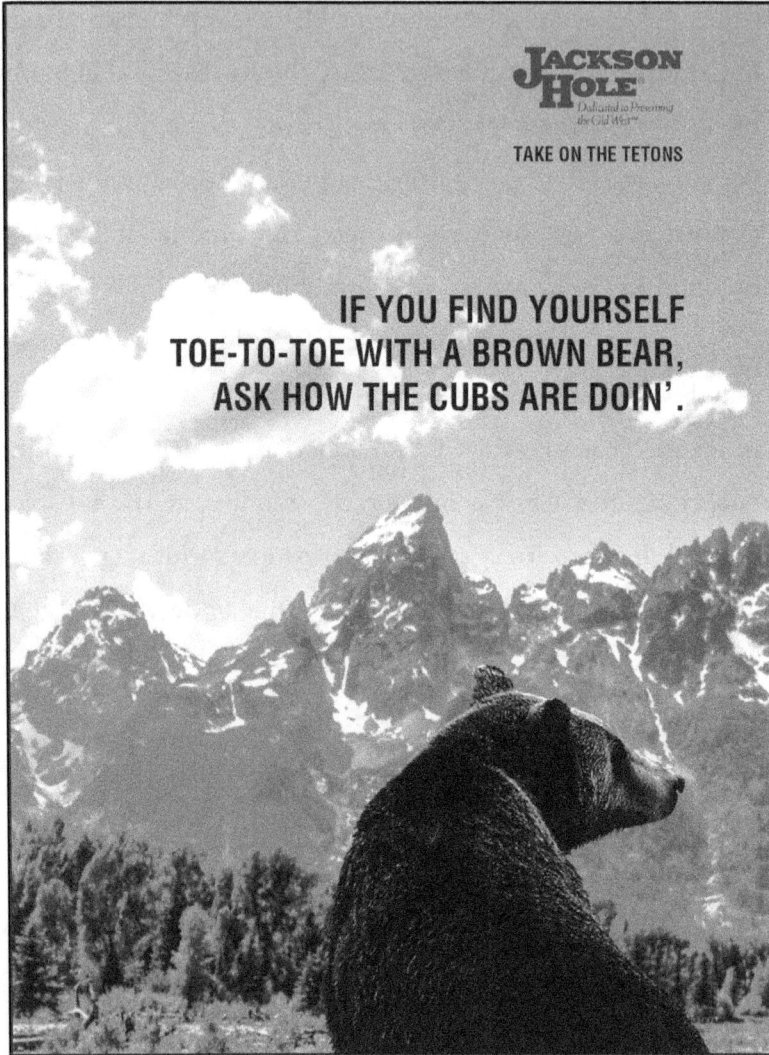

Competition Example 1 | Jackson Hole Mountain Resort - "Take On The Tetons." This Value variation of BIP 4 links the desire to connect with nature with the competitive advantage of seeing wildlife in the wild.

Competition Example 2 | Moto Guzzi motorcycles - "Aspire."
This Attribute variation of BIP 4 differentiates the Moto
Guzzi culture from the culture of less desirable brands.

Interactive Experience

The fifth big idea pattern is the *Interactive Experience,* in which the advertisement engages the viewer in a sensory approach, literally or figuratively involving the senses, i.e. seeing, hearing, tasting, smelling, and/or feeling. Interaction with the ad can stimulate the viewer, and promote the benefits of a product or service. Variations include: *Activation* and *Imaginary.* In the Activation variation, the viewer is engaged in a first-hand experience requiring physical activity and attentiveness. In the Imaginary variation, a concept engages the viewer's mind, inviting one to imagine an experience (Goldenberg, Mazursky, & Solomon, 1999). The formula is: State of Being (S) ± Interaction of Benefit (I) = Discovery (D), where variable States of Being (S_n) are linked with variable Interactions of Benefits (I_n) to arrive at new Discoveries (D_n). As an equation, BIP 5 looks like this: $S_n \pm I_n$ = Big Idea.

The Activation type of Interactive Experience big idea pattern is demonstrated in the following example: a sheet of apple-scented scratch-and-sniff stickers. In this example, one sticker may be cinnamon-apple-scented while another is caramel-apple-scented, etc. Additional scents could include absurd scents, for humor or dramatic effect. The Imaginary variation of this concept is identical, except in this case the viewer simply *imagines* the experience, as opposed to literally interacting with the medium in which the ad appears. The same scratch-and-sniff example could apply in the imaginary variation, perhaps with a tagline inviting the viewer to imagine the scents.

Two tangible brand campaigns are provided here to further illustrate BIP 5. The first example is a campaign for Breathe Right nasal strips, a product that provides relief in sinus conditions such as stuffy nose and snoring, so users breathe better and sleep better. The list of variable States of Being (S_n) includes: (S_1) breath-focused activities such as yoga; (S_2) marathon racing and sports requiring heavy breathing; (S_3) sleeping situations such as a bed at home... The list of variable Interactions of Benefits (I_n) include: (I_1) a billboard with an open space to allow air to flow through it; (I_2) origami instructions for folding a paper pinwheel to blow air through (activation interaction); (I_3) a maze game in which a rabbit escapes a snake through open passageways (imaginary interaction)... $S_n \pm I_n$ = Breathe Right sponsors a new roadway that dramatically improves the flow of traffic.

The second illustration of BIP 2 is a brand campaign for Montana Fresh and Local, an organic produce distributor. Here, the list of variable States of Being (Sn) includes: (S1) organic farming; (S2) pumpkin patches and corn stalks; (S3) roadside stands selling fresh produce... The list of variable Interactions of Benefits (In) include: (I1) free samples to taste the flavor (activation interaction); (I2) recipes to encourage people to try new vegetables (activation interaction); (I3) a color chart of fruits and vegetables red, orange, yellow... reminding people to eat all seven colors for a healthy variety (imaginary interaction)... Sn ± In = a harvest party with hands-on events such as berry picking, a cornfield maze, and/or vegetable toss" contests.

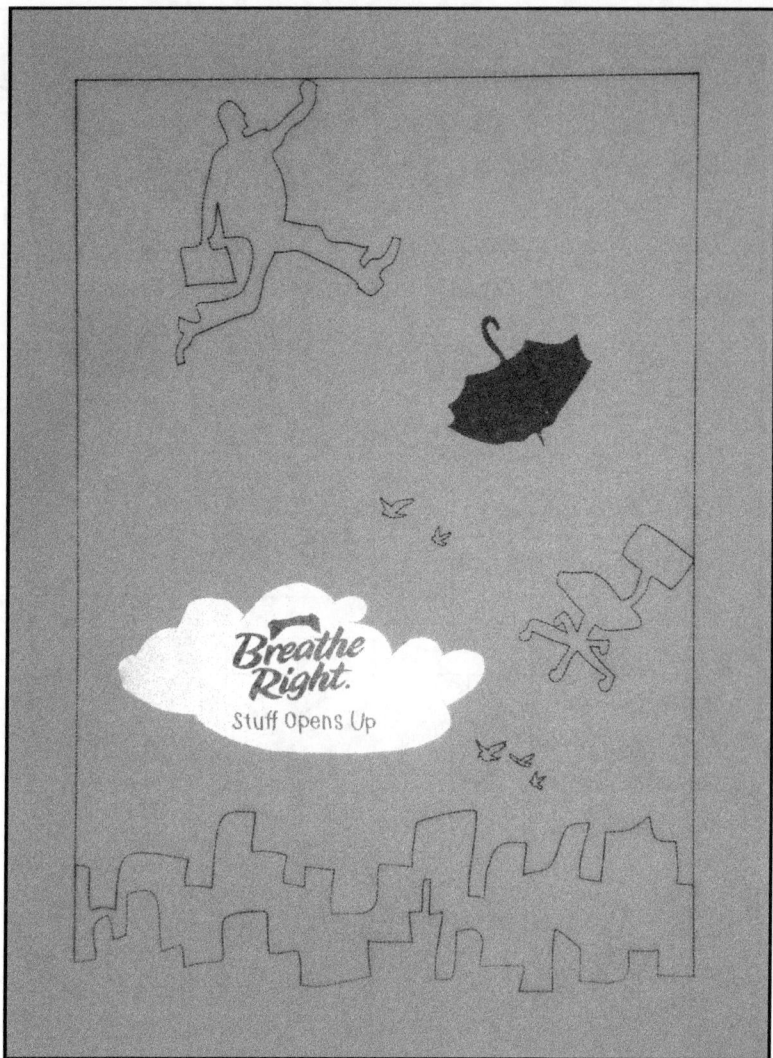

Interactive Experience Example 1 | Breathe Right nasal strips - "Stuff Opens Up." This Activation variation of BIP 5 has perforated edges, inviting viewers to punch out shapes and open up the ad itself, highlighting the main product benefit: opens up stuffy noses.

An Eggplant Named Sue

Interactive Experience Example 2 | Montana Fresh and Local organic produce - "An Eggplant Named Sue." This Activation variation of BIP 5 displays a comic strip in one frame per page of the Price & Availabilities catalog, encouraging produce managers to view the offerings completely.

Dimension Alteration

The last of the six big idea patterns is *Dimension Alteration*, in which the object is manipulated in relation to its environment. In all its variations, an ordinary situation is made entertaining by shifting the dimensions of the scenario, e.g. past/future, bigger/smaller, with/without, etc. There are four variations: *Multiplication, Division, Time Leap,* and *New Parameter Connection*. The first two variations involve altering the object's size or quantity, such as duplicating it or dividing it into its components. The Time Leap variation features the object's benefit in a way that is heightened through presentation in the past or future. Finally, in the New Parameter Connection variation, the object's parameter dimensions are altered, i.e. characteristics or elements (Goldenberg, Mazursky, & Solomon, 1999). The formula is: State of Being (S) ± Alteration of Benefit (A) = Discovery (D), where variable States of Being (Sn) are linked with variable Alterations of Benefits (An) to arrive at new Discoveries (Dn). Viewed as an equation, BIP 6 is: Sn ± An = Big Idea.

Examples of altered dimensions are as follows. In the Multiplication variation, a object could be multiplied into its enlarged state, e.g. an apple is turned into a horse carriage by the fairy godmother Granny Smith in order to transport Ciderella to the ball to meet Prince Braeburn. In the Division variation, an object is divided, e.g. an apple is split horizontally to emphasize its star-shape center and infer that the apple is a star. The Time Leap variation presents an ordinary situation involving the object, with a past or future twist, e.g. a dinosaur eats an entire apple tree all at once. In the New Parameter Connection variation, previously unrelated factors become related, e.g. the health quality of an apple is demonstrated by a zombie returning to life when an apple falls into a tomb.

Two tangible brand campaigns are provided here to further illustrate BIP 6. The first example is a campaign for Almond Joy candy bars. The list of variable States of Being (S_n) includes: (S_1) two morsels per package; (S_2) coconut filling; (S_3) milk chocolate coating... The list of variable Alterations of Benefits (A_n) include: (A_1) a planet where almonds stand on the foothills of chocolate mountains blanketed with snowy white coconut flakes (multiplication/division alteration); (A_2) medieval knight trying to open a candy bar with his sword (time leap alteration); (A_3) Kama Sutra positions are demonstrated by two chocolate morsels (new parameter connection alteration)... $S_n \pm A_n$ = an elderly couple with one morsel each, reflecting the moment they fell in love.

The second illustration of BIP 2 is a brand campaign for Steinway & Sons pianos. Here, the list of variable States of Being (Sn) includes: (S1) recital or concert; (S2) recording session; (S3) moving a piano up a staircase... The list of variable Alterations of Benefits (An) include: (A1) a tiny piano fit for a ladybug (multiplication/division alteration); (A2) a group of robots gathered around a piano performed by a human being (time leap alteration); (A3) Stevie Wonder performs on a piano and gains visions in vivid detail and color (new parameter connection alteration)... Sn ± An = a God-size piano in the sky where John Lennon performs alongside Beethoven.

154 CABE LINDSAY

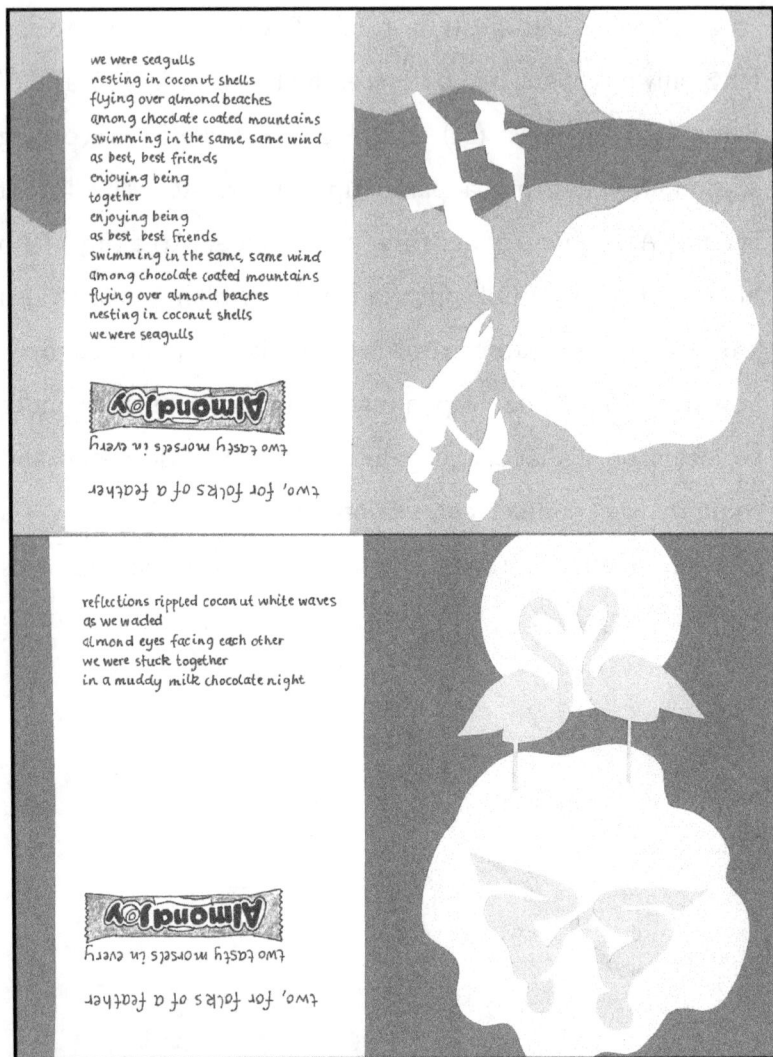

we were seagulls
nesting in coconut shells
flying over almond beaches
among chocolate coated mountains
swimming in the same, same wind
as best, best friends
enjoying being
together
enjoying being
as best best friends
swimming in the same, same wind
among chocolate coated mountains
flying over almond beaches
nesting in coconut shells
we were seagulls

two tasty morsels in every
two, for folks of a feather

reflections rippled coconut white waves
as we waded
almond eyes facing each other
we were stuck together
in a muddy milk chocolate night

two tasty morsels in every
two, for folks of a feather

Dimension Alteration Example 1 | Almond Joy candy bars - "Two, for Folks of a Feather." This Multiplication variation of BIP 6 features lovebirds reflecting upon lovebirds, highlighting the opportunity for sharing the candy bar with a loved one, since there are two morsels per pack.

Dimension Alteration Example 2 | Steinway & Sons pianos - "The Way." This Multiplication variation of BIP 6 exaggerates the magnitude of the sound, and suggests an elevation of a person's consciousness.

- - - - - - - - - - - -✂- -

Key Takeaways in Big Idea Patterns

- The "Metaphor" equation is formulated as follows: State of Being (S) ± Metaphor (M).

- The "Extreme Situation" equation is formulated as follows: State of Being (S) ± Extremity of Benefit (E).

- The "Results" equation is formulated as follows: State of Being (S) ± Results of Benefit (R).

- The "Competition" equation is formulated as follows: State of Being (S) ± Competitive Benefit (C).

- The "Interactive Experience" equation is formulated as follows: State of Being (S) ± Interaction of Benefit (I).

- The "Dimension Alteration" equation is formulated as follows: State of Being (S) ± Alteration of Benefit (A).

CHAPTER 9
BLOWING UP BIG IDEAS

"Many a small thing has been made large by the right kind of advertising." —Mark Twain

"Around here, however, we don't look backwards for very long. We keep moving forward, opening up new doors and doing new things, because we're curious... and curiosity keeps leading us down new paths." —Walt Disney Company

Big ideas have a tendency to explode when a creative professional takes dedicated action steps to light their fuses. Take the following big idea explosions, for starters: the historic first flight of an airplane, a computer in every home, and a protected environment—boom, boom, boom! The Wright Brothers' big idea: develop a reliable method of pilot control as the key to solving "the flying problem." Their action steps included numerous experiments with failed prototypes before building the first effective airplane, and made the historic first flight in 1903. Bill Gates' big idea: put a computer in every home and office. He creating an operating system and a set of powerful creative tools that blurred the line between work and play, resulting in the "personal computer." Julia Butterfly Hill's big idea: safeguard a 600-year-old redwood tree. She lived in the tree for 738 days straight, before vacating the tree when the lumber company agreed to preserve "Luna" and all trees within a 3-acre buffer zone.

To illustrate the spectrum of possibilities that opens up once an artist arrives at a big idea, let's consider Walt Disney's big idea: create entertainment that appeals to all age groups. Disney's actions in exploding this big idea included the invention of a career in animation, and the persistent pursuit of his artistic passion. His studios dipped into bankruptcy and then rocketed into riches; The Walt Disney Company is the world's largest media group in terms of revenue. Walt Disney is an innovator in animation and theme park design, as well as being the creator of some of the world's most beloved fictional characters. Disney's big idea grew into numerous executions, leaving a legacy that continues to grow: fictional characters, stories, movies, theme parks, games, and more.

The following items have one thing in common: Mickey Mouse, Disneyland, *Snow White and the Seven Dwarfs* (1937 film)—these all support Disney's big idea of entertainment that appeals to adults and children alike. Essentially, the Walt Disney Company is re-packaging this same big idea into different forms that reinforce the same big idea, thereby building a reputation of seamless "magical" experiences to its audience. This same principle exists in other creative professions: extend the vision into multiple executions of the same big idea. Successful brand campaigns follow this pattern, and countless authors, musicians, and artists do the same. The key in extending a big idea is a unified vision across different executions.

Integrated Marketing Communications

In the business world, the principle introduced above is called integrated marketing communications (IMC). The way IMC works is by communicating the same message across different communications channels—a campaign with one big idea, all supporting a single object with a unified message (Bendinger, 1993) (Needles, 2012). The two main benefits of IMC include: (1) making extra contact points with the audience; and (2) building resonance and recognition in the audience' mind. IMC avoids redundancy by echoing the message with subtle variance—differing media channel, refreshing the word choice, shifting the subject matter, etc.—while keeping the big idea intact.

IMC facilitates the expansion of a big idea inside and outside of the business world. At its pinnacle, a consumer's ordinary experience turns into an "artsperience," with familiar and comfortable artworks intermixed with daily life. Consider the following big idea: invite people to slice an apple horizontally, revealing the star-shape in the core, with the call-to-action: "Wish Upon An Apple." This idea might appear first in a street art poster pasted on a wall near a grocery store. The idea could continue with sticker labels placed on the apples in the produce aisle. The website wishuponanapple.com could be available to information-seekers. The website could link to YouTube, video demonstrating the horizontal apple slice technique, with discussion points made on Twitter, with the hashtag #wishuponanapple...

Street artists use public spaces as canvases to reach broader audiences than traditional art galleries and ad spaces typically allow, as seen in this large-scale interior mural painting.

The big idea is reinforced when an identical tone of voice carries it through all platforms: from the writing of a Google+ message to the writing of a blog post, from the performance of a flash mob to the performance of a sign thrower, and from painted brushstrokes to musical riffs. The possibilities for delivering big ideas is just as expansive as the possibilities for discovering big ideas. Non-traditional possibilities are immense as there is massive unexplored territory and room for growth. Street art, for example, can be painted, projected, or otherwise presented on the sides of buildings, buses, and bridges. Ambient platforms for big ideas commonly include areas of transit, such as installments by roadsides, in bus stops, and in subway systems, e.g. a gigantic apple sculpture in New York City serves as a symbol of local pride in "The Big Apple."

New media platforms invite the audience to participate in making a big idea bigger. Viral videos, blogs, games, and social networks are a few notable examples—each of these platforms facilitates peer-to-peer sharing. A television commercial, forcibly consumed, is easily transitioned to an online video, voluntarily consumed, shared on YouTube, for example (Porter & Golan, 2006). Branded viral videos like these can be viewed at will at any time, and shared as links. Similarly, websites and blogs facilitate sharing in an interactive way. Big idea-focused blogs are often emotionally-based, as opposed to traditional corporate websites which tend to be information-based, and each type has the option of inviting audience interaction. An example of a big idea in the form of a videogame is an "advergame," i.e. an interactive advertisement inviting consumers to essentially play with a big idea.

Future Art

Artists face five highly favorable conditions for future art: timeliness, awareness, community support, aspiration, and imagination. In terms of timeliness, the Creative Age will boost the interest and support of artists, and generate higher demand for creative services. In terms of awareness, life experiences combined with educational backing will send idea seekers sailing to new destinations, on new paths, through new books, toward new modes of thinking. Community support will invite artists to emerge into the public spotlight, where they can be seen in the open waters, riding waves of creativity alongside their collaborators. Their aspirations will send snorkelers and SCUBA divers deep into unfathomable depths of their creative juices, where their innermost ideas become reality. Their imaginations will bring them springing up from the blue, from the blue whales' blowholes, by golly. :)

---

1. *Timeliness* – Seeing the continuing rise in the value placed on creative services.

Creative thinkers are the most valued human resource today (Kluger, 2013) (Andrew, Manget, Michael, Taylor, & Zablit, 2010) and the value placed on creative services is expected to rise further (Florida, 2013) (Pink, 2006) (Bureau of Labor Statistics, 2010) (UNCTAD, 2010). If the predictions of Pink et al. prove true, then the public desire for right-brained thinking will exceed the desire for left-brained thinking, and there will be a greater need for creative services. With the increasing demand for creativity comes more opportunities for artists, more recognition, and a higher likelihood of success and achievement.

Truly, the world is currently turning in the artist's favor for the future. Strong evidence of this is the fact that technology is helping to level the artists' playing field. For example, independent artists can mass produce their artwork, if they desire to, with print-on-demand services that safeguard their investments. This commercialization model works for digital art, i.e. books and audio recordings, and nearly any artwork can be digitized. For analog artists, there are marketplaces for one-of-a-kind art too, e.g. Etsy, the "global handmade and vintage marketplace." For performance artists, there tools for promoting events, e.g. Facebook and Eventbrite.

Today's top talent is now measured by community curators, aided by tools like Digg and Facebook's "Like" button. New media enables creative participation, and when creative communities interact with art, the lines between artists and audiences blur—artwork inspires more artwork, karaoke brings singers to the spotlight, video games allow character creation... Audiences take an active role, rallying behind the art, investing in it, sharing it, and communicating about it as the "credible masses," collectively determining quality, thereby enabling creative professionals to get new opportunities based on the quality of their work.

As a result, remarkable talent is emerging in all creative genres, around the world. Proof is Ai Weiwei. Proof is Miranda July. Proof is Peter Donnelly, Marina Abramovic, Wes Anderson... Proof is the globalization of dance festivals and street art, both provocative and profitable. Proof is the success stories of independent authors, recording artists, and filmmakers. Proof is in the thriving "art films," e.g. *Being Elmo* and *The Tree of Life*. Proof is the fact that creativity now occurs in everyday life, and everyone everywhere is making creative decisions, which means we can all can let go of our old notions of artists as lone, tortured geniuses. Here and now, creativity is a simple, bare necessity of life. Creativity has changed. Creativity is normal now.

> 2. *Awareness* – Experiencing the world's richness in all its exotic flavors, and learning the rules in order to break them purposefully.

This creativity toolkit, and others, will empower creative professionals with tools that enable them to become keen innovators, problem-solvers, and creators. Explorations in ideation and artistry will add new tools to the toolset. Exercising the use of these tools will make artists prolific. With practice, creative professionals will improve in their artistic ability. When the creative blocks start to fall, prepared artists will reassemble the blocks like Legos into towers that bring them higher into their thought clouds, or bridges that lead them to greener pastures of art.

Good news: The human brain can change and improve with use. Although the human brain does not create new brain cells after birth, the brain can continue to grow dense, and this increased density is the result of "dendrites" that are created when we experience something new. Dr. Marian Diamond's research on the importance of schema shows that people who have captivating life experiences, such as music and travel, not only gain knowledge about the world, but also gain the ability to think at higher levels about that knowledge (Diamond, 1988). Awareness is a springboard for creativity—the more diverse one's knowledge is, the broader one's basis of intuition. This is supported by advertising thought leaders (White, 2002) (Ogilvy, 1983) (Sullivan) (Tellis & Ambler, 2007).

---

3. ***Community Support*** – Being connected in a social group with other artists who inspire.

Collaboration between different artists improves the chances of selecting the right solutions. Strength is gained in numbers, and when people work together for a common good, the effect is greater than the sum of their individual effects, i.e. synergy. For example, let's consider some of the visionary films that happen when two visionary artists collaborate: *Eternal Sunshine of the Spotless Mind*, with Charlie Kaufman and Michel Gondry; *Dancer in the Dark*, with Björk and Lars Von Trier; *Young Frankenstein*, with Gene Wilder and Mel Brooks...

Collaboration is easier than ever. Internet connectivity allows us to work with others no matter where we happen to be, even from the comfort of home, i.e. telecommuting. Crowdfunding platforms enable us to raise money to invest in our dreams, and social media platforms empower us to spread the word (O'Reilly & Milstein, 2009). Fostering connections is about synergistic collaboration, and also about discussing shared passions among likeminded people (Chayka, 2013). Both the artists and the audiences are participating in community engagement. Holistic art is emerging as a trend in the art world, and holistic marketing is advocated in business. Holistic communication invites audiences to take action, and play with the artwork on a conceptual level—stirring the emotions and then allowing and encouraging sharing, e.g. viral videos (Needles, 2012).

4. *Aspiration* – Pursuing some degree of success, primarily in terms of accomplishment and secondarily in terms of accolade.

Artists are motivated most by achievement (Ray & Anderson, 2000) (Rentel & Zellnik, 2007). Yes, the primary goal of any creative professional is to make good work (Chayka, 2013) (Barry, 2008) (Kilgour & Koslow, 2009) (Sullivan, 2008), and the success factor is of secondary importance. Success, however, can contribute favorably to an artist's ability to achieve. Historical examples of creative professionals whose artistic achievements grew with their success stories include: entrepreneurs, e.g. Henry Ford and Bill Gates; film makers, e.g. Charlie Chaplin and Steven Spielberg; writers, e.g. Stephen King and JK Rowling... Generally speaking, successful artists are able to do more with their creativity.

To optimistic artists, the world is full of adventures and opportunities to think and act creatively. Their positive attitudes lead them into passionate action, healthy risk-taking, and creative freedom—this behavior pattern is recommended as the road to success in creative professions (Foster, 2007) (SARK, 2004) (Griffin, 2008) (Cameron, 2002). Indubitably, when people follow their passions, they are more likely to think of new ways to overcome the challenges of life.

---

5. *Imagination* – forming mental sensations and trusting in the potential truth of them.

Just imagine the type of world we will create, when all of us are following our dreams. More of us will be dreaming, and the more we dream the more our dreams will come true. Most of us will be sporting tattoos, plus eco-friendly transportation, handmade clothes, and joyful noises. Street performance will flourish—yes, history's most common means for employment for entertainers will bloom like roses on roadsides. Comedy troupes will entertain traffic jams. Bluegrass jams will breakout among blue collar workers during their lunch breaks. Artists will apply clever brushstrokes to bare concrete. Actors and playwrights will play for change, in every way. Purely out of passion, hobby singer-songwriters will devote more time to their tunes, and professional rock stars will devote more of their wealth to good causes.

Public education will embrace creative thinking as an essential survival skill. Art teachers will become curators responsible for presenting the world that *ought* to be. Classrooms will be transformed into collaborative studios that facilitate open communication and expression between students and mentors. Ideation will be required learning, alongside fiction writing and filmmaking. High school graduates will be prepared to create and innovate in whatever paths they choose.

If trends continue, then songs will surpass diamonds in terms of their value, and ideas will become the common currency. Gangsters and hipsters will unite to stop the violence and start the violin lessons. Drum circles, artist collectives, and flash mobs will assemble, taking the place of police. New Bob Dylans and Marleys will emerge, alongside

Moondogs, Banksys, and Shakespeares, pushing the possibilities of music, theatre, visual art into new media, with new audiences, and new ways of showing and sharing appreciation. When art is appreciated, it will appreciate.

-----------✂---

Key Takeaways in Blowing Up a Big Idea

- A big idea tends to explode when dedicated action steps light their fuse.
- Success stories in big idea explosions include the ideas and actions of inventors, entrepreneurs, educators, environmentalists, artists...
- Integrated marketing communications (IMC) enables big ideas to explode by delivering a distinct vision across different platforms.
- Excellent platforms for blowing up a big idea include:
  o Ambient – reaching the audience in areas of mass transit, e.g. bus stops
  o Interactive – enabling sharing and inviting consumers to play with a big idea
- Five favorable qualities of future artists include: timeliness; awareness; community support; aspiration, and imagination.

CHAPTER 10
CONCLUSION

The big idea is the most important manifestation of creativity. In any outlet for creative expression, the success or failure of an artwork is rooted in the presence or absence of a big idea. The concept is more important than its execution. The substance is more important than the style (Barry, 2008). While the impact of an artwork is potentially enlarged through integrated marketing communications—and other tactics designed to reach the masses—the big idea itself is the key to an artwork's impact. In the absence of a big idea, nothing is made bigger. A device is just a device, without a big idea. A gimmick is just a gimmick. But a big idea stands on its own regardless of its execution quality or its mode of delivery.

The two definitive qualities of a big idea are sensibility and surprise, appealing to both sides of the audiences' intellect. While some creative professionals favor left-brain or right-brain thought processes, the advertising profession celebrates a balance of both: creativity and logic. Achieving a big idea requires dual-competency in originality and appropriateness, and these qualities are fundamental to an idea that is considered valuable. Appropriateness is a logical, left-brain aspiration, while originality is right-brain pursuit that invites complete randomness and pure chance. Big ideas live in the crossroads between the two: the place where surprising newness and understandable relevance intersect.

The path of successful creative professionals is illuminated by a comparison between advanced artists and beginners. The creative process differs greatly between professionals and beginners. For example, beginners tend to be self-limiting, ruling out ideas, overly concerned by the details of the execution. Advanced artists open themselves to more possibilities—their tendency is free-flowing and unfiltered ideation. Advanced artists generate a higher quantity of ideas, and this increases the likelihood of reaching higher quality ideas. Advanced artists further deepen their search for big ideas by including an "adaptation" phase to develop their more viable ideas. These differences show that creative processes tend change with experience.

Academic studies and professional testimonies reveal behaviors, techniques, and resources that can help creative professionals to be more idea prone. Recommended behaviors include risk-taking, spontaneity, improving self-image, and believing in success. Recommended ideation techniques include the formal brainstorming method, concept cross-tabulation, and others, exercising both left-brain and right-brain mind-frames. The resources recommended here are introduced with this guidebook for the first time. These are the big idea patterns: power tools for creativity. The six big idea patterns demonstrate step-by-step formulas for discovering big ideas.

Big ideas can be strategized and executed more efficiently with more impact, on budget and on time, through awareness and practice of advanced creative processes. This book highlights some of the empowering behavior patterns, techniques, and resources—shortcuts that enable creative professionals to improve their ability to discover big ideas. The challenge of discovering big ideas on demand is solved by a streamlined, systematized creative process. Roy Spence, co-founder of the Austin-based advertising agency, GSD&M, writes, "Visionary ideas are discovered, not created" (Sullivan, 2008). By this, he refers to the fact that big ideas in advertising are rarely attained through spontaneous breakthroughs in clarity. Instead, big ideas are earned through a dedicated search for answers: a process.

GLOSSARY

Art Director: A person who is responsible for the selection, execution, production, etc., of graphic art for a publication, advertising agency, or the like.

Big Idea: A contribution to a brand image in an original and appropriate way.

Big Idea Pattern (BIP): A creative resource designed to facilitate focused creativity, which leads to effective outcomes.

Brainstorming: A group technique of solving specific problems, amassing information, stimulating creative thinking, developing new ideas, etc., by unrestrained and spontaneous participation in discussion.

Client Brief: A short, concise informative statement shared between a client and its agency, ensuring that the agency is on-target when providing its service to the client.

Concept Cross-Tabulation (CCT): The process of developing a brand by analyzing two categorical variables in order to reach unforeseen associations with significant meaning.

Convergent Problem-Solving: The method used to generate the correct, logical answer to standard questions that do not require creativity.

Copywriter: Writer of copy for advertisements.

Creative (n.): A creative person, esp. one who devises advertising campaigns.

Creative Brief: A document used by creative professionals and agencies to develop creative deliverables incl. visual design, copy, advertising, websites, etc.

Creative Director: The person responsible for overseeing all aspects of branding and advertising.

Creativity: The phenomenon whereby a person creates something original and appropriate as a way to smartly address complicated problems for the benefit of a client.

Divergent Problem-Solving: The method used to generate creative ideas by exploring many possible solutions.

FCB Planning Grid Explosion: A technique of visualizing a brand from the consumers' perspective and using that as the basis to explore new possibilities for a brand, with new insights revealed.

Freelancing: The act of working as a writer, designer, performer, or the like, selling work or services by the hour, day job, etc., rather than working on a regular salary basis for one employer.

Headline: A prominent line of large, bold text designed to arouse interest and curiosity about the advertised product or service.

Ideation: The process of generating new ideas and forming messaging to support these ideas in words and images.

Integrated Marketing Communications (IMC): A management concept that is designed to make all aspects of branding cohesive, working together as a unified force throughout advertising, sales promotion, public relations, and other marketing communications aspects.

Microsite: A website that is intended for a specific limited purpose and is often temporary.

Mind Mapping: A technique of diagramming used to represent words, ideas, or other items linked to and arranged around a central key word or idea. Mind maps are used to generate, visualize, structure, and classify ideas, and as an aid to studying and organizing information, solving problems, making decisions, and writing.

Mindscribing: A technique of transcribing one's thoughts during the creative process as a method for building a database of words, sketches, phrases, and associations that would fuel ideation.

Morphological Matrix: A structured ideation technique that incorporates a grid, yielding answers to a challenge.

Storyboarding: An ideation technique that serves as a visual outline of thoughts.

Synectics: A technique of identifying and solving problems that depends on creative thinking, the use of analogy, and informal conversation among a small group of individuals with diverse experience and expertise.

Tagline: A memorable phrase that sums up the tone and premise of an advertisement, used to reinforce the audience's memory of a product.

Viral Video: A video that becomes popular through the process of Internet sharing, typically through video sharing websites, social media, and email.

REFERENCES

American Association of Advertising Agencies. (2007).
Agency Advertiser Value Survey: 1-34.

Andrew, J.P., Manget, J., Michael, D.C., Taylor, A., & Zablit,
H. (2010). *Innovation 2010: A Return to Prominence—
and the Emergence of a New World Order*. Boston, MA:
The Boston Consulting Group.

Ashley, C., & Oliver, J. D. (2010). Creative Leaders: Thirty
Years of Big Ideas. *Journal of Advertising*, 115-116.

Barry, P. (2008). *The Advertising Concept Book: A complete
guide to creative ideas, strategies and campaigns*. New
York, NY: Thames & Hudson Inc.

Beverland, M., Farrelly, F., & Woodhatch, Z. (2007). Exploring
the Dimensions of Proactivity within Advertising
Agency-client Relationships. *Journal of Advertising,
36(4)*, 49-60.

Bendinger, B. (1993). *The Copy Workshop Workbook*.
Chicago, IL: The Copy Workshop.

Boojihawon, D.K. (2007). Network Dynamics and the
Internationalization Process of Small Advertising
Agencies. *Service Industries Journal, 27(6)*, 809-829.

Bureau of Labor Statistics, U.S. Department of Labor. (2010). *Occupational Outlook Handbook, 2010-11 Edition.* Retrieved 9/7/13 from http://bls.gov/oco/

Calantone, R.J., & Drury, D.H. (1979). Advertising Agency Compensation: A Model for Incentive and Control. *Management Science, 25(7),* 632-642.

Cameron, J. (2002). *The Artist's Way: A Spiritual Path to Higher Creativity.* New York, NY: Tarcher/Putnam.

Chayka, K. (2013). *The Biggest Tip to Succeed as an Artist: Be Open.* Retrieved 9/7/13 from http://hyperallergic.com/65604/the-biggest-tip-to-succeed-as-an-artist-be-open/.

Clapperton, G. (2009). *This is Social Media: Tweet, Blog, Link and Post Your Way to Business Success.* West Sussex, UK: Capstone Publishing.

Cleveland, B. (2008). Here are Four Ways to Build the Trust it Takes to Keep Your Clients Around. *Advertising Age, 79(9),* 16-16.

Creativity. (n.d.). In *Wikipedia.* Retrieved 9/7/2013, from http://en.wikipedia.org/wiki/Creativity

Dart, J. (1980). The Advertising Agency Selection Process for Small Business: Tips from the Agencies. *Journal of Small Business Management, 18(2),* 1-10.

Davies, M.A.P. (2006). Developing a Model of Tolerance in
Client-agency Relationships in Advertising.
International Journal of Advertising, 25(3), 381-407.

Diamond, M. (1988). *Enriching heredity: The impact of the
environment on the anatomy of the brain.* New York,
NY: The Free Press.

Florida, R. (2012). *The Rise of the Creative Class--Revisited
(2nd edition).* New York, NY: Basic Books.

Foster, J. (2007). *How to Get Ideas.* San Francisco, CA: Berrett-
Koehler Publishers, Inc.

Fox, D. (2010). *Ad Value: Workflow Efficiency on Large Scale.*
TVB Europe, 18-19.

Frazer, C. (1983). Creative Strategy: A Management
Perspective. *Journal of Advertising, 12(4),* 36-41.

Going With the Flow. (2009). *SHOOT, 50(8),* 19-20.

Goldenberg, J., Mazursky, D., & Solomon, S. (1999). The
Fundamental Templates of Quality Ads. *Marketing
Science, 18(3),* 333-352.

Goldenberg, J., & Mazursky, D. (2002). *Creativity in Product
Innovation.* Cambridge, MA: Cambridge University
Press.

Goodwin, L.M. (2005). Workflow Optimization Cuts Costs At
Deutsch Advertising. *Seybold Report: Analyzing
Publishing Technologies, 5(13),* 8-13.

Graphic Artists Guild. (2007). *Graphic Artists Guild Handbook: Pricing & Ethical Guidelines*. New York, NY: Graphic Artists Guild.

Griffin, W.G. (2008). From Performance to Mastery: Developmental Models of the Creative Process. *Journal of Advertising, 37(4)*, 95-108.

Haag, C., & Coget, J.F. (2010). Leading Creative People: Lessons from Advertising Guru Jacques Seguela. *European Management Journal, 28(4)*, 278-284.

Halinen, A. (1997). *Relationship Marketing in Professional Services – A Study of Agency/Client Dynamics in the Advertising Sector*. New York, NY: Routledge.

Halliday, J. (2006). Toyota to Saatchi: Move Forward. *Advertising Age, 77(4)*, 1-29.

Hameroff, E.J. (1998). *The Advertising Agency Business: The Complete Manual for Management & Operation (3rd edition)*. Chicago, IL: NTC Business Books.

Harris, J., & Taylor, K.A. (2003). The Case for Greater Agency Involvement in Strategic Partnerships. *Journal of Advertising Research*, 346-351.

Jaffe, A. (2003). *Casting for Big Ideas: A New Manifesto for Agency Managers*. Hoboken, NY: John Wiley & Sons, Inc.

Johar, G.V., Holbrook, M.B., & Stern, B.B. (2001). The Role of Myth in Creative Advertising Design: Theory, Process and Outcome. *Journal of Advertising, 30(2),* 1-25.

Jones, J.P. (1999). *The Advertising Business: Operations, Creativity, Media Planning, Integrated Communications.* Thousand Oaks, CA: SAGE Publications, Inc.

Kilgour, M., & Koslow, S. (2009). Why and How Do Creative Thinking Techniques Work? Trading Off Originality And Appropriateness To Make More Creative Advertising. *Journal of the Academy of Marketing Science, 37(3),* 298-309.

Kitchen, P.J., Kim, I., & Schultz, D.E. (2008). Integrated Marketing Communications: Practice Leads Theory. *Journal of Advertising Research, 48(4),* 531-546.

Kluger, J. (2013). Assessing the Creative Spark: What Americans think about creativity. *Time, 181(19),* 58.

Koslow, S., Sasser, S., & Riordan, E. (2006). Do Marketers Get the Advertising they Need or the Advertising they Deserve? Agency Views of How Clients Influence Creativity. *Journal of Advertising, 35(3),* 81-101.

Krieff, A. (1993). *How to Start & Run Your Own Advertising Agency.* New York, NY: McGraw-Hill.

Law, A. (1999). *Creative Company: How St. Luke's Became "The Ad Agency to End All Ad Agencies."* Hoboken, NJ: John Wiley & Sons, Inc.

Lockett, D.M. (1980). *Guide to Getting New Business Leads.* Chicago, IL: Crain Communications, Inc.

Loori, J.D. (2004). *The Zen of Creativity: Cultivating Your Artistic Life.* New York, NY: Ballantine Books.

Lupton, E., & Phillips, J.C. (2008). *Graphic Design: The New Basics.* New York, NY: Princeton Architectural Press.

McAlister, L., Srinivasan, R., & Kim, M. (2007). Advertising, Research and Development, and Systematic Risk of the Firm. *Journal of Marketing, 71(1),* 35-48.

McNamara, J. (1990). *Advertising Agency Management.* Homewood, IL: Dow Jones-Irwin.

Minsky, L. (2007). *How to Succeed in Advertising When All You Have is Talent.* Chicago, IL: The Copy Workshop.

Morais, R.J. (2007). Conflict and Confluence in Advertising Meetings. *Human Organization, 66 (2),* 150-159.

Mumford, M.D., Hunter, S.T., & Byrne, C.L. (2009). What is Fundamental? The Role of Cognition in Creativity and Innovation. *Industrial & Organizational Psychology, 2(3),* 253-256.

Needles, A.B. (2012). *Balancing the Demand Equation.* Danville, CA: New Year Publishing, LLC.

Ogilvy, D. (1983). *Ogilvy on Advertising*. New York, NY: Crown Publishers, Inc.

O'Reilly, T., & Milstein, S. (2009). *The Twitter Book*. Sebastapol, CA: O'Reilly Media, Inc.

Patterson, F., Kerrin, M., Gatto-Roissard, G., & Coan, P. (2009). *Everyday Innovation: How to enhance innovative working in employees and organizations*. London, UK: NESTA.

Pink, D.H. (2006). *A Whole New Mind: Why Right-Brainers Will Rule the Future*. New York, New York: Penguin Group.

Porter, L. and Golan, G. (2006). From subservient chickens to brawny men: A comparison of viral advertising to television advertising. *Journal of Interactive Advertising, (6)2*, 30-38.

Pricken, M. (2008). *Creative Advertising: Ideas and Techniques from the World's Best Campaigns*. London, England: Thames & Hudson.

Rangaswami, A. (2009). The Formula for Success. *Media: Asia's Media & Marketing Newspaper*, 28-28.

Ray, P.H., & Anderson, S.R. (2000). *The Cultural Creatives: How 50 Million People Are Changing The World*. New York, NY: Three Rivers Press.

Rentel, R., & Zellnik, J. (2007). *Karma Queens, Greek Gods, and Innerpreneurs: Meet the 9 Consumer Types*

Shaping Today's Marketplace. New York, NY: McGraw-Hill.

Reynolds, J. (2008). Digital Agency Production Workflows Are Now. *SHOOT, 49(15),* 3-3.

Riveong, D. (2007). *ROI & Integrated Campaigns: Commoditizing the Client-Agency Relationship?* Retrieved 9/7/13 from http://www.emergence-media.com

Russell, J.T., & Lane, W.R. (1996). Kleppner's Advertising Procedure. Englewood Cliffs, NJ: Prentice Hall.

Salovey, P., Brackett, M.A, & Mayer, J.D. (2004). *Emotional Intelligence: Key Readings on the Mayer and Salovey Model.* Port Chester, NY: National Professional Resources, Inc.

Sanders, L. (2004). Communication Key. *Advertising Age, 75(17),* 100-100.

SARK. (2004). *Make Your Creative Dreams Real: A Plan for Procrastinators, Perfectionists, Busy People, and People Who Would Really Rather Sleep All Day.* New York, NY: Simon & Schuster, Inc.

Sasser, S.L., & Koslow, S. (2008). Desperately Seeking Advertising Creativity. *Journal of Advertising, 37(4),* 5-19.

Schaughnessy, A. (2005). *How to Be a Graphic Designer without Losing Your Soul*. New York, NY: Princeton Architectural Press.

Sims, M. (2004). *Agency Account Handling – Avoiding Blood, Sweat and Tears*. West Sussex, England: John Wiley & Sons, Ltd.

Smerczek, R. (2009). Client Bonding: Try Improv. *Brandweek, 50(17)*, 18-18.

Smith, R.E., & Yang, X. (2004). Toward a General Theory of Creativity in Advertising: Examining the Role of Divergence. *Marketing Theory, 4(12)*, 31-58.

Sullivan, L. (2008). *Hey Whipple, Squeeze This (3rd edition)*. Hoboken, NJ: John Wiley & Sons, Inc.

Sutherland, J., Duke, L., & Abernethy, A. (2004). A Model of Marketing Information Flow – When Creatives Obtain and Want to Know Clients. *Journal of Advertising, 33(4)*, 39-52.

Tellis, G.J., & Ambler, T. (2007). *The SAGE Handbook of Advertising*. Thousand Oaks, CA: SAGE Publications, Inc.

UNCTAD. (2010). *Creative Economy Report 2010*. Retrieved 9/7/13 from http://unctad.org/en/Docs/ditctab20103_en.pdf

Van Camp, S. (2003). BBDO Goes Tapeless. *Adweek Magazine's Technology Marketing, 23(5)*.

Verbeke, W., Franses, P.H., Le Blanc, A., & Van Ruiten, N. (2008). Finding the Keys to Creativity. *Journal of Advertising, 37(4)*, 121-130.

Vitrano, R. (2008). Marketers, Agencies, it's Time to Play Nice in the Sandbox. *Advertising Age, 79(2)*, 14-15.

Webber, E. (2007). Big Agencies Could Learn A Thing Or Two From Us. *Advertising Age, 78(31)*, 23-23.

West, D.C., Kover, A.J., & Caruna, A. (2008). Practitioner and Customer Views of Advertising Creativity: Same Concept, Different Meaning? *Journal of Advertising, 37(4)*, 35-45.

White, G. (1977). *John Caples: ADMAN*. Chicago, IL: Crain Communications, Inc.

White, S.P. (2002). *New Ideas about New Ideas: Insights on Creativity from the World's Leading Innovators*. Cambridge, MA: Perseus Books.

Ziegler, S.K., & Johnson, J.D. (1981). *Creative Strategy and Tactics in Advertising: A Managerial Approach to Copywriting and Production*. Columbus, OH: Grid Publishing, Inc.

BIG IDEA PATTERNS
CREATIVITY TOOLKIT

About the Author

Cabe Lindsay is an author with works including children's literature, a fiction novel series, and a full-length album of original songs. He describes his big idea as follows: "In my experience as an art director, I've found that the secret to a successful campaign is to find clarity first. For me, clarity comes when I sit quietly, with closed eyes and an open mind. Instead of frantically tossing around ideas, or firing keystrokes and mouse clicks, or doodling on a sketchpad, I aim for the opposite—I become a human being instead of a human doing. Here, in the stillness, I listen for the voice of my superconscience, whom I call The Youniverse, while the layers of clouds drift away." See CabeTV.com.

About the Book

Big Idea Patterns is a creativity toolkit for the discovery and launch of sensible, sensational ideas that resonate. The book originated as a professional report, submitted in 2010, required for completion of a master's degree in advertising from The University of Texas. The report was subsequently published by LAP LAMBERT Academic Publishing on September 26, 2011 under the title: *Big Idea Patterns of the Advertising Creative Process: A Brainstorming Toolkit for the Discovery and Launch of Sensible, Sensational Campaigns that Resonate.* The book you are currently reading improves upon the original in terms of its readability, elaboration, and examples. All iterations of this book are designed to simplify the creative process, enabling artists with the tools that can help them to realize their big ideas. See BigIdeaPatterns.com.

About the Publisher

Big Idea Patterns is published by Ahstin™, an independent publishing house. Ahstin is a creative services studio specializing in ideation (idea formulation, education, and creation). In simple terms, Ahstin helps people to: (1) get their ideas out; and (2) do something with them. Specific solutions include creativity coaching programs with custom-tailored brainstorm sessions to support all sorts of creative endeavors. For example, business managers can navigate confidently through the fog of a campaign. Artists can stretch their imaginations. Inventors can innovate by improvising, collaborating, and refining ideas. Clients include art directors, writers, recording artists, entrepreneurs, city planners, university professors... See Ahstin.com.

www.ingramcontent.com/pod-product-compliance
Lightning Source LLC
LaVergne TN
LVHW051830080426
835512LV00018B/2808